D0195175

GOD

IS THE ISSUE

Yours for making God the issue,

Brad Bright

BRAD BRIGHT

REVISED

Bright Media
FOUNDATION

God Is the Issue: Recapturing the Cultural Initiative

Published by
Bright Media Foundation
Campus Crusade for Christ
375 Highway 74 South, Suite A
Peachtree City, GA 30269

First Edition © 2003, Second Edition © 2008, Brad Bright. All rights reserved. No part of this book may be reproduced, stored in a retrieval system, or transmitted in any form or by any means, except in the case of brief quotations printed in articles or reviews, without prior permission in writing from the author.

Design and production by William Graham Agency

Cover by Left Coast Design

Edited by Brenda Josee, Cindy Peach, and Micki Griffith

Additional Layout and Editing by Steve Tyrrell / Tyrrell Creative

Printed in the United States of America

ISBN 1-56399-243-4

Unless otherwise indicated, Scripture quotations are from the *New International Version*, © 1973, 1978, 1984 by the International Bible Society. Published by Zondervan Bible Publishers, Grand Rapids, Michigan.

Scripture quotations designated TLB are from *The Living Bible,* © 1971 by Tyndale House Publishers, Wheaton, Illinois.

This book is dedicated to the man who has made the God of the Bible the issue wherever he has gone for more than fifty years. From him I learned that one's perspective on all of life's issues, big and small, is colored by one's view of God. And today, I too believe with everything inside me that God is the single issue upon which all of life hinges. I dedicate this book to the greatest man I have ever known, or ever expect to know—my father.

Contents

*In focusing on effects (immoral behavior), we allow
the true Cause of moral behavior (God Himself) to be
sidelined in the debate, and thereby end up arguing over
symptoms. In a relativistic "Just do it!" culture, "Thou
shalt not..." cannot compete.*

*Three reasons are given for why the church is losing the
battle for the heart, soul, and mind of the culture: we lack
compassion, boldness, and training. The church is chal-
lenged to exchange its "sword for a fishing pole."*

*Practical and biblical examples are used to illustrate how
to make God the issue. Examples are given of how Jesus
aggressively co-opted the rhetoric of His opponents.*

Acknowledgments

I want to thank Michael Richardson for his help with research and his creative, fertile mind that could not think inside the box even if he so desired. I am grateful to Jim Bramlett for his research. My thanks to William Kruidenier for helping me shape my words. I owe a great debt of gratitude to Alan Sears and Richard Jefferson at the Alliance Defense Fund for keeping me out of trouble. And a world of thanks to my friend and associate John Nill who has graciously coached me through this process.

But there are two people to whom I owe my greatest thanks. The first is my late father, Bill Bright, who over a period of months convinced me that I needed to write this book. Without his encouragement I would have never begun the process. The second is my beloved bride, Kathy, whose tremendous patience, understanding, listening skills, and encouragement gave me the time, space, and daily feedback I needed to effectively formulate my thoughts on paper. She deserves as much credit as I for this book.

Foreword

One afternoon just prior to 9/11, my younger son, Brad, dropped by the house. Sitting at the kitchen table we began chatting as we often do. And as is pretty typical in our family, the conversation soon moved to a discussion of the current state of our American culture. Our two sons, Zac and Brad, spent their growing up years exposed to a constant stream of national and world visitors through our home, listening to and participating in dialogue about God and the needs of the world around us. Now that the boys are grown and have their own families and ministries for our Lord, little has changed when we sit down together. Zac brings the thoughtfulness of a pastor/philosopher, while Brad injects the viewpoint of a former political activist now ministering with Campus Crusade for Christ.

This particular day I was exercised afresh about the terrible tragedy of the 1973 *Roe v. Wade* Supreme Court decision, which has resulted in the murder of approximately 40 million innocent unborn babies. I have several times proposed to have myself lashed to the pillars of the Supreme Court building until that horrendous ruling is rescinded. (I have never followed through with that action largely due to my beloved wife, Vonette, who shares my views concerning the evil of abortion but prayed with me for a better solution.)

"But Dad, abortion is not the real issue," Brad said.

The puzzled look on my face was an invitation for him to

continue: "Abortion is just a symptom. God is the issue! Abortion, homosexuality, active euthanasia, and pornography are all just symptoms. We have let others set the agenda for us. They have framed the debate and we have been foolish enough to accept their terms of engagement. We must reframe the entire rhetorical playing field in order to make God the issue within the culture."

As Brad continued to flesh out his thoughts, the light went on! Why had I not thought of this before? As a nation, our spiritual blood has been poisoned, yet we are merely treating the boils that have resulted. In order to cure a sick culture, we must attack the root cause: the exclusion of God from American culture. "You must write your ideas down," I said to Brad.

In the months following that initial conversation, I continued to urge him to commit his ideas to writing and refine them into book form. I consider them important enough for every leader in America who follows Jesus Christ to consider. Much of what our Founding Fathers put in place still stands—a free press, individual liberty, a market economy, and so on. But without question, the greatest difference between the America of 1776 and the America of 2003 is the banishment of the God of the Bible—the God of Abraham, Isaac, and Jacob; the God and Father of our Lord Jesus Christ—from the public square. *To that fundamental flaw in the fabric of our modern culture can be traced the weakening of every moral seam since.* Only by restoring God to His rightful place as the central issue in all of human life—political, spiritual, moral, economic, philosophical—will there be sufficient motivation and reason to correct what ails America.

In the following pages Brad demonstrates the absolutely

critical distinction between focusing on morality and focusing on the *source* of morality in the public square—the God of the Bible. Morality is only a symptom. God is the cause. The question we must ask ourselves is whether or not we are content to merely suppress cultural symptoms such as abortion, with varying degrees of success, or whether we really wish to cure the underlying disease. How we answer this question has major implications for how we expend our time, energies, and resources.

There are three reasons I am pleased to commend Brad's book to you: First, it is a message both Brad and I believe is from God Himself, nurtured in Brad's heart and confirmed in mine during years of observing godlessness from one coast to another in our country. Whether working with political leaders in Washington, D.C., or debating anti-God radicals on the university campus, Brad's conviction that God is the issue has grown deep roots and borne abundant fruit.

Second, the message of *God Is the Issue* is eminently biblical, and a message for our times. While wishing I had enjoyed Brad's insights fifty years ago in my own ministry, I can rest in the fact that God raises up His spokesmen (and spokeswomen, like Esther) to come to the kingdom "for just such a time as this." I believe this book is a sorely needed paradigm message for America, and that it comes providentially at this time.

Third, every Christian can and should apply this approach when tackling the tough moral, spiritual, and political issues facing our nation. Paradigm shifts do not happen overnight. But the progress we make in thinking, and therefore acting, biblically about this subject will determine the kind of culture our children and grandchildren will inherit from us.

We need not settle for a "post-Christian America," or yield to the relentless onslaught against the God whose followers were instrumental in founding this great nation. As Ezekiel saw the dry bones of Israel come back to life before his eyes, we can see the soul of America revived by restoring God to His rightful place in our land—in our hearts, on our lips, in our homes, in the boardroom, in the classroom, in the marketplace, in the public square, and in the halls of government.

Brad and I are praying that God will place it upon the hearts of leaders to intentionally influence tens of millions of our fellow Americans to once again make the God of the Bible the watershed issue within our culture. It is our desire that America will *soon* say again with sincerity and authenticity, "In God we trust." Learning to attack the cause instead of the symptoms of moral and spiritual decay will require a reprogramming for today's Christian community. We are counting on you to be a part of this God-ordained movement for His glory and praise as we seek to help our fellow countrymen once again discover the God of the Bible.

Founder, Campus Crusade for Christ, Int'l

Introduction

There are moments in life when we must face reality, ask the tough questions, and then choose a new course of action. I believe American Christians are at one of those crossroads in the history of our nation. The strategies of the past few decades to recapture the culture are not getting the job done. We are losing the battle for the hearts and minds of our fellow countrymen.

This book was conceived in the fall of 1992 as I sat in a pew at Hollywood Presbyterian Church listening to Dr. Lloyd Ogilvie (who went on to serve eight years as the Chaplain of the United States Senate before retiring in March 2003). His sermon that day was entitled "The Answer is God." For years I reflected on the meaning of what he said that day, and I too have come to the conclusion that the answer is God—both in street-level practice and in theory. He is the answer to every dysfunction I face as an individual, and He is the answer to every dysfunction we face as a society. If there is no God, then the questions of life are truly meaningless. In the words of King Solomon of ancient Israel, "Utterly meaningless! Everything is meaningless" (Ecclesiastes 1:2). God really is the only issue.

Since the nation's founding, many churches across America have preached consistently about the person of Jesus Christ. That history has been punctuated by several periods of preaching on various and sundry social ills. During the decades since the moral upheaval of the 1960s, we have seen an increase in that kind of preaching again. And yet, despite our preaching, as we begin the new millennium we are confronted with a society that is shamelessly attempting to shake off all remaining vestiges of decency and morality. Society has removed God from His place at the center of everything and given Him a seat on the sidelines. And we as the church have acquiesced to their agenda, and have joined the debate over symptomatic issues instead of clarifying that God is the logical and necessary starting point for all cultural debates.

The church in America today generally communicates with the culture in one of two ways. Either we preach the straight gospel without regard to the cultural and personal context, or we simply react defensively to the symptomatic cultural ills—such as homosexual behavior, abortion, racism, or pornography. Unlike Jesus, we have a difficult time using the cultural context as a relevant platform for making the God of the Bible the issue. Therefore, God comes across as largely irrelevant to the everyday life of the average American. Consequently, the culture ends up regarding us (along with the God of the Bible) as out of touch or, worse, dangerous.

In light of this, if the Bible is true, and the God of the Bible really exists, we must conclude that we have failed to effectively communicate "God" to our culture.

My hope is that we can learn to use the symptomatic "felt" issues within our culture as springboards to address what underlies the cultural mindset in which we live and breathe—our God-belief (or lack of it). What we believe to be true about God will determine how we live and relate to those around us.

Let me say parenthetically, this book is not written for the person who intends to hold frank and open dialogue regarding the pros and cons of certain types of symptomatic behavior within the culture, such as homosexuality, premarital sex, abortion, racism, pornography, or euthanasia. Nor is it written for the person who needs to learn how to explain to his non-Christian neighbors the basics of how they may know God personally. It is not even written for the individual who is seeking to further develop an intimate relationship with God. Of course, we need to know how to do all of these things, but that is not the purpose of this book.

This book is written to the person who ardently desires to bring about wholesale change within the American cultural mindset. It is written to the person who wishes to help frame the message that could ultimately allow us to win the war, not just individual battles. It is written for the person who wants to put the "Cornerstone" (God Himself) back into His proper place as the foundation upon which the American social and moral experience will be erected once again.

It is not my intent to denigrate those who have opposed evil and fought valiantly for what is right. In fact, I applaud you and thank you from the depths of my heart and encourage you to persevere. However, despite winning many battles, we are still losing the war for the hearts and minds of our countrymen. The nation in which I am now raising my children bears more resemblance to the Sodom that Lot knew than to the America in which my father was reared. Stemming the tide is no longer enough. *We must either thrust back the tide or acknowledge defeat.* Such an effort demands a radical new plan whose elements are as old as history itself.

The bottom line is this: we need a game plan that distinguishes between cause and effect. In that process, we need tactics that allow us to foil and frustrate the opposition by using their own tools and words against them—much like Jesus did with the Pharisees. It is time to return to the basics, but in a more culturally relevant and understandable manner. Only then will we be able to ultimately win the culture war, by making the God of the Bible the central issue within the culture. Debating the issues apart from the larger context of God Himself is the practical equivalent of rearranging the deck chairs on the Titanic while it sinks beneath the waves. There is no longer any other way to win.

My desire is that this book will help us all along that path— laypersons, pastors, visionaries, strategists, ministry leaders, businessmen, and politicians. I hope it will help us frame the "God" issue in a way that our fellow Americans can more readily understand and accept. I trust it will help us to recapture the soul of America so that we may become the "shining light on a hill" that was the dream of our forefathers. I pray that, along with the sons of Issachar in 1 Chronicles 12:32, we too may understand our times and know what to do.

CHAPTER 1

IDENTIFYING CAUSE AND EFFECT

"If there is no God then everything is permitted."
—*Fyodor Dostoevsky*

Amererica, the noble experiment, is under siege. The nation that once aspired to being a shining light on a hill is now one of the world's leading exporters of pornography. The nation that was once a haven for religious refugees now seeks to exclude religious speech from education and the public square. The nation that once paid the blood price to free its slaves now freely spills the blood of its young on the altar of "choice." Religious belief, once revered, is now publicly reviled. The foundation of all that most of us once held dear as a nation has so eroded that it can no longer stay the culture.

Many have worked diligently in the public square for almost three decades in order to hold back the tide of evil in America. We all owe those individuals a great debt of gratitude and our continuing support. My prayer is that God will continue to strengthen their hands for the tasks He has given them. However, every year that goes by we continue to lose more ground. For every step we take forward, we seem to take two steps back. So then a natural question arises, "Why?"

Recently, a friend made a comment to me that I have taken to heart, "The first step in bringing about change is to be brutally honest with yourself." Honestly, the current strategy of promoting morality without re-establishing the source of morality is not working. Not only has American culture not improved over the last 25-30 years as Christians have actively engaged in the public square, but it has actually worsened.

The primary remedy is not simply to restore "traditional values." Although it is helpful, it is no longer enough. As a nation we have gone so far down the road of moral relativism that the foundation that once supported traditional morality is now largely eroded. Values, while very important, are merely symptoms, or effects. Therefore, we must not only attempt to restore values, but must deal with the underlying cause of their erosion, otherwise our efforts are ultimately wasted.

In light of this I would like to ask the following questions:

1) What was the lead issue addressed by the very first amendment to the Constitution in the Bill of Rights[i]? Given the intellectual prowess of the Founding Fathers do you think this was by chance or intentional? Why do you think the Founding Fathers listed it first, even before freedom of speech?

2) What kind of speech have the "intellectual elites" such as the ACLU virulently and consistently assailed over the years in an overt attempt to drive it from the public

---

[i]The first amendment to the Constitution of the United States says: "Congress shall make no law respecting an establishment of religion, or prohibiting the free exercise thereof; or abridging the freedom of speech, or of the press; of the right of the people peaceably to assemble, and to petition the government for a redress of grievances."

square? Why do you think this is?

3) Which came first: court rulings suppressing religious speech and removing prayer from public schools, or rulings legalizing abortion and sodomy? Why?

4) What is the connection between a person's belief in God and their behavior? If God does not exist, what can you point to in the universe that *OBLIGATES* me to respect your rights and not trample all over you if I perceive such action to be in my best self-interest? In other words, how is the concept of morality divorced from God any more real than the idea of the Tooth Fairy, Santa Claus or the Easter Bunny?

The father of our country, George Washington, understood the answer to these questions very well as reflected by his statement:

> *Reason and experience both forbid us to expect that national morality can prevail in exclusion of religious principle.*[1]

He also said:

> *It is impossible to rightly govern the world without God and the Bible.*[2]

Our first President knew that the basis of morality is God specifically, the God of the Bible. Without Him, "national morality" cannot prevail, because there will be no rational foundation to support it.

The words of our second President, John Adams, are also profound:

> *Our Constitution was made only for a moral and religious people. It is wholly inadequate to the government of any other.* [3]

If Washington and Adams were correct in their assessment, those concerned about the moral state of our society need to take the next logical step in order to effectively turn the battle. We must become skilled at distinguishing between cause and effect. We must begin focusing more of our efforts on curing the disease instead of just trying to suppress the cultural symptoms. If we fail in this regard, it will be to our own detriment both as individuals and as a nation.

Some have already begun to understand this while many still have not. Following the September 11, 2001 attacks on the World Trade Center and the Pentagon, some of our religious leaders laid the blame at the feet of the homosexuals, radical feminists, abortionists, pornographers, and other misguided groups of blind sheep. However, on September 13, two days after the bombings, Jane Clayson on CBS's *The Early Show* interviewed Anne Graham Lotz, the daughter of Billy Graham. Jane asked her, "If God is good, how could God let this happen?" Anne's response nailed the problem dead center:

> *For several years now Americans in a sense have shaken their fist at God and said, "God, we want you out of our*

BELIEVING IN
MORALITY WHILE
DENYING GOD'S
EXISTENCE IS
NO DIFFERENT
THAN BELIEVING
IN THE TOOTH
FAIRY.

schools, our government, our business; we want you out of
our marketplace." And, God, who is a gentleman, has just
quietly backed out of our national and political life, our
public life, removing His hand of blessing and protection. [4]

Anne's response reflected a clear understanding of the difference between *cause* and *effect*, between disease and symptom. She understood that the core issue is our nation's rejection of the God of the Bible from the public square. God has given us free will. If we want to kick Him out of our house we can do that. However, one of the consequences is He will no longer be there to protect us. If we do not welcome God into our house today, then how can He be there to protect us when trouble comes knocking tomorrow?

Many years ago, Margaret Sanger, the founder of Planned Parenthood, articulated the difference between cause and effect:

Birth control appeals to the advanced radical because it
is calculated to undermine the authority of the Christian
churches. I look forward to seeing humanity free someday
from the tyranny of Christianity. [5]

Sanger's ultimate goal was not to promote birth control. Rather, she ardently desired to "undermine" the authority of the church in a "calculated" manner. Birth control was merely the means, the vehicle, the tool. The end game was undermining belief in the God of the Bible.

Aldous Huxley, author of *Brave New World,* sheds additional light why many people are so intent on removing God from our culture in his book *Ends and Means:* "The philosopher who finds no meaning in the world is not concerned exclusively with a problem in metaphysics. He is also concerned to prove that there is no valid reason why he personally should not do as he wants...." [6] Aldous Huxley may have said the words, but Adolph Hitler and Joseph Stalin gave them their horrific and logical expression.

The damning and prophetic words of Aleksandr Solzhenitsyn, spoken three decades ago in an address over the BBC radio network, have come back to haunt us. Accusatorially summing up the mentality of the West during the 20th century, he stated, "Since there are no higher spiritual forces above us and since I—Man with a capital M—am the crowning glory of the universe, then if anyone must perish today, let it be someone else, anybody, but not I, not my precious self, or those who are close to me." [7] We have pushed God aside and focused on self. And as we have pragmatically focused on self, we have lost the unpragmatic ability to "love our neighbor"—a necessary element of morality. (It is no accident that Jesus said, in Matthew 22:35–40, that the two universal laws on which all others hang are, first, to love God, then to love one's neighbor. If there is no God, then there is nothing in the universe that obligates me to love my neighbor as myself.

It is now time to recognize with Anne Graham Lotz, Aleksandr Solzhenitsyn, and many others that *moral collapse is not the critical issue.* It is no more than a symptom of a much deeper problem. Therefore, to allow abortion, homosexual behavior, or any other moral issue to continue to dominate the primary debate is akin to focusing on patching the cracked walls of a building constructed on a crumbling foundation. A discerning person will quickly correct the problem with the foundation. Otherwise he will be patching the walls right up to the day that the foundation finally gives way and the entire structure collapses—patches and all.[8]

When my child comes to me with a skinned knee, a Band-Aid is a good solution. When a friend is diagnosed with heart disease, a Band-Aid is no longer adequate. America now has heart disease. Treating the symptoms is no longer enough.

In the Bible, Jesus told the story of two men. One man built his house on a foundation of rock, the other man built his house on sand. One house withstood the storms, the other collapsed (Matthew 7:24–27). Trying to restore "traditional values" or "biblical values" in our nation without restoring the foundation of those values is like the man who built his house on a foundation of sand.

We must begin rebuilding the foundation by making the God of the Bible the central issue of life in the minds of those around us. He must become the dividing line of the culture. Not everyone must believe in the God of the Bible. Not everyone must be a follower of Jesus or believe the Bible is true. But the God of the Bible must become the issue on which everyone has a strongly felt opinion. This will allow us to control the rhetorical playing field. And as any good debater understands, if you can control the rhetorical playing field, you are almost guaranteed victory in the end. Both the apostle Peter and the apostle Paul modeled this for us in the Book of Acts as they made Jesus the primary issue wherever they went. Like them, we dare not be ignored on this one issue. To be ignored necessarily means failure.

To be sidetracked ultimately means defeat. If we fail at this task, we will ultimately fail to reverse the moral slide of society.[9]

If we continue to solely debate "behavior" in the current cultural vacuum of moral relativism, we cannot win the culture war. We will win some battles due to the pragmatic nature of many of our arguments, but never the war. For instance, pragmatism often helps us to promote abstinence because it is clearly the most effective means of preventing unwanted pregnancies and sexually transmitted diseases. However, it hurts us in opposing stem cell research on human embryos. Pragmatism says that because they are going to be discarded anyway, we should use those embryos for research to try to help other people.[10] Although being pragmatic is often effective, we must be ever mindful that pragmatism is a fickle ally.

We must face the reality that in most cases our argument does not "feel" as good. In a relativistic culture, "Thou shall not…," cannot compete with, "Just do it!" Even the Bible is clear that sin is pleasurable for a time (Hebrews 11:25). Why would people deny themselves a single pleasure if, from their perspective, the God of the Bible really does not exist or is irrelevant to everyday life?

However, switch the starting point of the cultural debate from behavior to God and victory becomes a real possibility. This is because it is rationally impossible to begin with the premise "God" (as defined by the Bible) and end with the conclusion that any immoral behavior is acceptable. Why else has the other side worked so hard to remove God from the public square, beginning with public education?

Let me illustrate. While ministering with Campus Crusade

> To assert that moral absolutes can exist
> without a rational basis in the universe is
> intellectual suicide.

for Christ at the University of Washington, our student leaders decided to hold a debate on moral relativism. I went to one of the professors in the Philosophy Department who was known to be an atheist to ask if he would debate the position that moral absolutes do not exist. After he finished laughing at me, he said that even though moral relativism is the philosophy of the masses, no philosophy professor who had any brains would debate in support of it because it was an intellectually bankrupt theory. I was absolutely shocked to hear this statement from a secular philosophy professor who was a known atheist! He advised me to go to the Literature Department where I should have no problem finding a "wacko" who would gladly take up the cause.

But the most profound statement he made is that "absolutes are self-evident." By this he clearly meant that moral absolutes must exist in the universe. However, his problem was that he had been unable to develop a rational argument justifying the existence of absolutes apart from God. Of course, this is always the insurmountable problem for those who have an inadequate or nonexistent God-concept. To say that absolutes exist in the universe divorced from any source (ex nihilo) is simply a form of intellectual suicide. "God" really is our trump card.

However, I do not believe that we can approach the process of talking about the God of the Bible in the traditional manner and expect to succeed. God-fearing people have worked hard to stem the tide of evil and yet abortion is firmly entrenched. Racism still pervades society, including the Church. Tolerance reigns supreme in the university. The active euthanasia movement advances under the mantra of "death with dignity." Pornography continues to tighten its death grip on us (according to James Dobson, about 40 percent of all U.S. pastors are addicted to pornography[11]). And homosexuals are trying to obliterate the already damaged concept of marriage by gutting it of any last vestiges of real meaning.

Bible believing Christians have become increasingly marginalized and irrelevant to the culture. Some leading pro-morality activists have in effect said that we have lost, so we should just take our toys, go home, and ride out the storm. Even Aleksandr Solzhenitsyn withdrew from the public arena in order to write for future generations since in his opinion we had already lost the culture war with no hope of regaining the advantage in our lifetimes.

The ultimate debate is about changing society's view of God, not modification of societal behavior.

The situation is bleak and the current strategy is not sufficient. *We need to develop a new game plan. We need a new set of blueprints. We need a different map.*

Two final points of clarification are needed here. First, we must keep in mind that the ultimate debate is not about changing societal behavior. Rather, it is about changing society's view of God. As a culture and as individuals, our behavior will necessarily be determined by our underlying God concept.

Second, many would say that the Church in America is faithfully proclaiming the Word of God thereby making God the issue. But if that is true, why do only 9 percent of all "born again" teens believe in absolute moral truth? (That means 91 percent of "born-again" teens do not believe in absolute moral truth.[12]) Why do 40 percent believe that Jesus sinned?[13] Why do 68 percent not believe that the Holy Spirit is real?[14] Why do 53 percent believe that all faiths teach equally valid truths? [15] Why do 78 percent of all students in private religious schools consider it acceptable to cheat on exams?[16] Why do 95 percent think it is okay to lie to their parents? [17] If American teens who have grown up in the church had a proper view of God, we would not see such statistical symptoms. Based on this and much more data, we can reasonably conclude that the Body of Christ today has failed to effectively communicate biblical truth about God—at least to young people (and the research on adults is not much more encouraging). This is true for a number of interrelated reasons, which we will explore in the next chapter.

In this regard, Oswald Chambers writes in *My Utmost for His Highest,* "Conscience is that faculty in me which attaches itself to the highest that I know, and tells me what the highest I know demands that I do. It is the eye of the soul which looks out either towards God or towards what it regards as the highest, and therefore conscience records differently in different people."[18]

If you still have any remaining vestiges of doubt about the cause and effect relationship between our view of God and our behavior, let me take the next few paragraphs to see if I can finally convince you beyond a shadow of a doubt that either we make God the issue or we will ultimately fail on every other front.

Philosopher, Friedrich Nietzsche anticipated our situation today in 1882 when he wrote of the madman who said:

> *"God is dead...And we have killed him.... Is not the magnitude of this deed too great for us? Shall we not ourselves have to become Gods, merely to seem worthy of it?"*[19]

But then the madman realizes that his listeners do not understand the implications of what they have done and so he continues:

> *"I come too early...I am not yet at the right time. This prodigious event is still on its way, and is traveling—it has not yet reached men's ears. Lightning and thunder need time, the light of the stars needs time, deeds need time, even after they are done, to be seen and heard. This deed is as yet further from them than the furthest star—and yet they have done it themselves!"*[20]

Nietzsche's unmistakable implication was that the Christian God is now "dead" in the minds of Western man but we yet have to recognize that the culture based upon belief in God's existence is also dead and must eventually be replaced by that which we must create for ourselves.

Nietzsche saw what was coming, but Tammy Bruce, a lesbian and author of *The Death of Right and Wrong,* describes what has now come: "Welcome to a culture where right and wrong have taken such a beating they're no longer recognizable. If you think this debasement of our culture can never really affect you, think again. Today's moral relativism and selfish agendas are moving through the body of society like a cancer, putting all of us at risk."[21] This is an out-of-the-closet lesbian saying this, not some "religious fanatic." She describes moral relativism (morality divorced from absolutes/God) as an aggressive fatal disease. Welcome to the 21st century.

You learn more about people's moral and political behavior if you know their image of God than almost any other measure.

Sam Harris, generally regarded as the founder of the New Atheist movement, summed it up best, "the big war is not between evolution and creationism, but between naturalism and supernaturalism."[22] His goal in the next two decades is to so profoundly impact culture as to make it socially and culturally unacceptable to publicly admit you believe in God by getting atheists to come-out-of-the-closet just as the homosexuals have done.

Finally, in 2006, Baylor University published an extensive study on religious belief in America. Here was Dr. Christopher Bader's conclusion based on his involvement with the study: "...you learn more about people's moral and political behavior if you know their image of God than almost any other measure."[23] If that is true, then the one thing we need to change in order to change people's moral and political behavior is their view of God since the two are inextricably connected.

Our view of God will determine our belief system as individuals and as a society.

Do you believe that the key to solving America's cultural problems is to make God the issue, or do you still have doubts? Do you still believe that if we just tried a little harder or tweaked things a bit here or there that we could turn the cultural tide? I believe that such thinking is akin to playing the game Whack-A-Mole. Whacking at symptoms may produce a short-term fix giving us more time, but whacking down symptoms will never make them go away and stay away.

I am convinced that our view of God will determine our belief system as individuals and as a society. It will determine whether we believe in "sexual preference" or the sanctity of God-ordained marriage. Will I demand "my rights," or do I fulfill my God-given responsibilities toward others? Do I talk about "death with dignity" or life with transcendent meaning? Is it merely a fetus, or is it a person created by God in His image? Will we, in the sarcastic words of Friedrich Nietzsche, "cry at the grave of God,"[24] or will we with the shepherds and the wise men bow at the manger? That is our choice as individuals. That is our choice as a society.

God is the central issue of all life, and therefore our view of God is the central issue for each of our lives as individuals, and for our culture. If we fail to make God the issue, we shall most certainly and inevitably fail on every other cultural front. Time is not on our side and neither is the culture. If we fail to make God the issue now, even greater personal sacrifice will be required in the future.

Chapter 1 Review Questions

1. George Washington said, "It is impossible to rightly govern the world without God and the Bible." What results do you see in our culture of attempting to govern America without the influence of God and the Bible?

2. Apply Washington's statement to your personal life. What differences do you see when you allow God and the Bible to "govern" your life? Why does national moral health begin at the personal, individual level?

3. In your own words, describe the difference between focusing on symptoms and focusing on causes. Why are discussions about symptoms irrelevant if there is no discussion about cause?

4. List five problems America faces which are symptomatic of a failure to acknowledge God. For each problem, identify the aspect(s) of God's character which have direct bearing on this issue.

5. What have you done in the past, or what can you do in the future, to make God the main issue in your life? In your community? In your state? In our nation?

CHAPTER 2

COMMUNICATING GOD'S HEART

"For God so loved the world that he gave..."

—*Jesus (John 3:16)*

Today, although the doors of the churches in this nation are still wide open, we are losing the battle for the hearts and minds of our fellow Americans. I believe this is true for a number of reasons, but I will address only three in this chapter.

Lack of Compassion

First, our hearts often do not truly reflect God's heart. We focus on symptoms, but God focuses on the cause. We tend to judge others based on their outward appearance. God always judges based on the heart.

A few years ago, a friend of mine, John (not his real name), was having problems in his marriage. One day his pastor stopped by unannounced and in no uncertain terms made it clear that John needed marriage counseling. After hearing what his pastor had to say, John explained the true problem: he was not following God closely and no amount of marriage counseling would do any good until he decided to put God first in his life. He rebuked the pastor for not having even asked about his spiritual condition. John instinctively understood that a person cannot follow Jesus Christ and at the same time be consistently self-centered—the primary cause of his marital troubles. I suspect the pastor was reminded that day of the importance of looking beyond the symptoms.

I have to keep this in mind myself. When I was younger, I was extremely judgmental of people who engaged in certain types of immoral behavior. In fact, I was clear that I wished those people would just go away forever. I now cringe inside as I recall this because my words certainly did not come from the God of the Bible who said, "Love your neighbor." Nor did they reflect the words of Jesus in the story of the Good Samaritan. Fortunately, a number of years ago, a long-time family friend gently pulled me aside and gave me wise counsel. He graciously complemented me on having a clear understanding of "right and wrong." Then he said, "But, Brad, you do not have the gift of compassion. Whatever you do in life, surround yourself with people who have the gift of compassion and ask for their counsel." In retrospect, I understand what he was saying with great diplomacy was I did not have God's heart. I did not even begin to grasp God's overwhelming compassion for all of humanity. Jesus Christ died for everyone. Who did I think I was to wish that anyone would die in his sins—and spend eternity in hell separated from his Creator?

My former lack of compassion for the lost is unfortunately not uncommon in the church today. I wish I could say that among those who claim to follow Jesus such thinking is rare. But sadly, I cannot. I wish I could say that my fellow Christians really embraced in their heart of hearts the sentiment, "Hate the sin, but love the sinner." But sadly, I cannot. I wish I could say that we live out the command, "Love your enemies. Do good to those who hate you." But sadly, I cannot.

A number of years ago, after my wife and I moved to a new city, we began looking for a church home. One Sunday we visited one of the more prominent churches in the area. That particular morning the pastor related how he had been out sailing the previous week with friends. Upon returning to the dock at the end of the day, he observed a rather weather-beaten character sitting on the dock reading his Bible. However, on closer inspection he saw a cigarette dangling from the man's mouth. And then, when a boat being removed from the water slid off its trailer and scraped on the concrete ramp, the man spewed forth a string of expletives.

At this point my mind raced to the story in the Book of Acts where Philip was sent by the Spirit of God out into the desert; there he crossed paths with an Ethiopian royal official who was reading the Scriptures without understanding, just as the man on the dock appeared to be. Recognizing this, Philip explained the Scriptures to him, and after the man embraced Jesus as God's son, Philip baptized him.

However, to my absolute shock, the pastor told his people that he walked away from the profane man burning with anger as he went. He looked down at the congregation, full of "righteous indignation," giving vent to his outrage, berating any in the sanctuary who might exhibit similar behavior. I was stunned. Not only had this pastor missed a tremendous opportunity to encourage a person in his search for God, but he had taught his congregation to focus on symptoms rather than the cause.

The next week we returned to the same church only to hear

the pastor tell another story about a drunk driver who had killed a mother and her child that past week. His words were scathing as he heatedly condemned the man. Once again, I felt as though someone had sucker-punched me. Yes, the drunk driver had done a horrible thing for which he should be punished by the state. However, a person who had just inadvertently killed a mother and her child would probably be in the midst of intense emotional distress, and therefore incredibly open to receiving God's forgiveness—if he only understood how.

We reject people because they are sinners. Yet that is exactly why they need God's forgiveness—because they are sinners.

I can only wish that the pastor had asked for volunteers from the congregation to go with him to minister to the man with "a cup of water" in the name of Jesus during his time of self-inflicted anguish. It would have been a natural moment to communicate God's incredible love and mercy. Another opportunity missed.

I am sure this pastor meant well, but just as we are all prone to do, he focused on suppressing the symptom rather than confronting the underlying cause. All of us, Christians and non-Christians alike, need to experience God's unconditional love and forgiveness because of our sins. That is what gives us hope. Through this forgiveness we receive the life of Christ—the foundation for real change, both individually and corporately.

> It would be one thing if the world hated us because they saw Jesus in us. However, I fear we are often hated because they do not see Jesus in us at all.

Is it any wonder that the world hates Christians? We often speak of God's condemnation, while neglecting to extend His love and forgiveness. We reject people because they are sinners. Yet that is exactly why they need God's forgiveness—because they are sinners. Let us never forget that we too have sinned. Even the apostle Paul claimed to have been the "worst of sinners" (1 Timothy 1:15,16). Jesus came to heal the sick, not the healthy. He came to seek and to save the lost. Jesus also told us to take the log out of our own eye first before we try to take the speck out of someone else's (Matthew 7:3–5). It would be one thing if the world hated us because they saw Jesus in us. However, I fear we are often hated because they do not see Jesus in us at all—rather they see only self-righteous "Pharisees" all too eager to cast the first stone. We should heed the words of Jesus when He accused the religious leaders of His day of being "hypocrites" and "whitewashed tombs, which look beautiful on the outside but on the inside are full of dead men's bones" (Matthew 23:27).

In Revelation chapter 2, Jesus commends the church in Ephesus because their deeds were great, they worked hard, and they did not tolerate wickedness in their midst; yet He had a complaint against them: they had left their "first love" for Him. Jesus said that the entire Law and the Prophets hang on the two commands to love God and love others (Matthew 22:37–40). The apostle Paul is very clear that if we do not have love, our deeds amount to nothing at all from God's perspective:

> *If I speak in the tongues of men and of angels, but have not love, I am only a resounding gong or a clanging cymbal. If I have the gift of prophecy and can fathom all mysteries and all knowledge, and if I have a faith that can move mountains, but have not love, I am nothing. If I give all I possess to the poor and surrender my body to the flames, but have not love, I gain nothing (1 Corinthians 13:1–3).*

Whenever God gives me the privilege of mentoring believers, I make it very clear that they will hear very little about behavior, but a lot about having a heart for God. Is this because behavior is unimportant? No! In fact, behavior is extremely important because it is an effective indicator of where the heart is. I watch behavior carefully (including my own), because behavior always follows belief. If behavior does not begin to change over time, there is usually still a heart problem that needs to be addressed. Simply put, I prefer to focus on treating the cause rather than the symptoms.

The pastor of the church we now attend is a lot like Philip in the Book of Acts. He is a man who has God's heart, and distinguishes between cause and effect. One Easter Sunday a few years ago, as the crowds were waiting to enter the church, he observed a number of people cursing and smoking. Instead of taking offense, he got excited because he knew such behavior was an indicator that there would be many in the audience that day who needed to hear that God loves them unconditionally and offers forgiveness—and he would have the privilege of explaining to them how they could receive it.

> Although God's condemnation is very real,
> His love is absolutely overpowering.

What a contrast! On the one hand is the pastor I mentioned earlier who focuses on outward behavior and condemns not only the sin but also the sinner. On the other hand is a pastor who understands what the outward behavior really means—it is merely a symptom. Although God's condemnation is very real, His love is absolutely overpowering. God's heart's desire is for reconciliation, not condemnation. That must be our heart's desire also.

Lack of Boldness

This leads to the second reason why we are losing the battle for the souls of our fellow citizens. In the church today, we spend the majority of our time sitting around the campfire, holding hands, and singing "Kum Ba Yah." We often forget that we are also to stand up and march out singing "Onward Christian Soldiers." (I mean this metaphorically, of course.) Most of us do not even attempt to communicate with the culture. We mistakenly (or conveniently) think it is the job of preachers and "full-time" Christian workers to evangelize.

While at the University of Washington, one of my fellow team members went to the student body president and asked him if anyone had ever taken a few minutes to explain to him how he could know God personally. The president responded by saying, "No, a number of my friends have had the opportunity but no one has ever taken it." (In other words, he knew that a number of his friends were Christians, but none of them had ever bothered to tell him how to begin a relationship with God.) His response reflects one of the primary problems we face in the church today: More often than not, we fail to even attempt to engage the culture in dialogue about who God is.

More often than not, we fail to even attempt to engage the culture in dialogue about who God is.

Once a young Christian I was mentoring told me that evangelism was just a "Campus Crusade for Christ thing." He said it certainly was not a directive for all believers. After I picked up my jaw off the floor, I suggested that we do a study of the Book of Acts. A few weeks later the young man sheepishly acknowledged that he had been wrong. It was a joy to see him begin to blossom as he followed the example of Peter, Paul, and even Jesus Himself taking advantage of opportunities to tell his peers about God's love and forgiveness.

Over the years I have had many people say to me, "Your father must have the gift of evangelism." Frankly, I am not convinced that he did. But I am convinced that he had God's heart of compassion for those who do not know the Creator God. When he received a telephone call that was a "wrong number," he told the caller about Jesus. He talked about Jesus to taxi cab drivers, CEOs, bag boys, flight attendants, hotel maids, doctors, nurses, criminals, lawyers, and politicians. Growing up, whenever we went on family vacations, we would often realize Dad was missing and turn around to see him talking with someone we had passed twenty yards earlier. It is important to understand that this was a man who was rather reserved by nature. He was not an extrovert by anyone's account. But he wanted people to know the God that he knew.

One of the worst excuses I have heard for not even attempting to tell others the good news about God's love is the statement, "I do not have the gift of evangelism." If such an excuse is legitimate, then I should be excused from having to show compassion since I do not have that "gift" (as I mentioned earlier). I am sorry if this comes across as offensive, but it needs to be said. *If we are not willing to talk about the one issue that is foundational to morality itself, we have no right to complain as the moral state of the nation continues to disintegrate.*

Lack of Training

The third reason we are losing the battle for the heart of America is this: Even when we do step outside our comfort zone and tell others about God's love, most of us do not know how to effectively communicate with our non-Christian peers. We often use words like "grace," "salvation," "born again," "sinner," or even "Christian." These are all good words if properly understood, but in many cases we might as well be speaking ancient Hebrew to our fellow citizens. When we move out of the church into the culture and we continue to speak our "in-house" language, it is not only unintelligible to the unchurched, but it can make them feel like outsiders. They cannot understand us, and therefore we are ineffective messengers.

While in politics in Washington, D.C., I remember asking an associate if he was a "Christian." Because of his Southern Bible-belt background he responded, "Of course, I am! What do you think I am, a Communist?!" With my West Coast up-bringing, it had never occurred to me that someone would really think in those terms. I have since learned that "Christian" can have a number of perceived meanings in our culture, a few of which are not even remotely positive—or accurate. And if the word "Christian" is misunderstood, do we really think words like "sin" or "salvation" are going to be properly understood?

If I want to communicate with Brazilians, I learn to speak Portuguese. If I want to address a businessman on Wall Street, I use illustrations from the world of finance and wear a conserva-tive suit. If I want to communicate with young children, I keep my vocabulary and choice of topics simple. When we do not understand our audience, we will at best fail to communicate. At worst, we can even come across as stupid, unloving, mean-spir-ited, intolerant, or hateful—despite our good intentions. Part of being a good messenger is learning how to shape our message so our audience can understand us. (I will deal with this more extensively in the following chapters.)

A few years ago, my wife and I lived next door to two ho-mosexual men, Bill and Rob. They were nice guys and we would chat with them as occasion permitted. One evening as I was working in the garage, Bill stopped by after work to talk. Know-ing I was a Christian, he started making statements clearly try-

IF WE ARE NOT WILLING TO TALK ABOUT THE ONE ISSUE THAT IS FOUNDATIONAL TO MORALITY ITSELF, WE HAVE NO RIGHT TO COMPLAIN AS THE MORAL STATE OF THE NATION CONTINUES TO DISINTEGRATE.

ing to provoke a negative reaction. However, I simply turned to him and graciously asked, "Bill, are you a Christian?" He looked at me a bit perplexed and then emphatically responded, "No!" To which I calmly replied, "Then I won't expect you to act like one." His behavior was not the primary issue, and he needed to understand that so we could then move to the underlying causal issue—his view of God.

Attempting to correct wrong behavior while ignoring a person's underlying view of God is shortsighted and ultimately destined to fail.

Once, while I was single, I went out of town for a few days and returned to discover I had left raw ground beef on the counter. It was full of disgusting, wriggling maggots and the stench was overwhelming. I often think of that experience as I observe the moral decay of our culture. If meat is left out on the counter, should I be surprised when it rots? If a blind person bumps into me, should I be surprised or offended? Of course not! Likewise, if a person does not believe in the God of the Bible or has a misconception about who God is, why should I be surprised when he behaves as if the God of the Bible does not exist? That person is merely behaving in a manner consistent with his very nature.

In the church we often confuse the symptom with the disease—the effect with the cause. We condemn a pagan for behaving like a pagan. Why would we expect a pagan to act any other way? Instead, we must help effect a change in that person's view of God. If this occurs, then his outward behavior should naturally change over time to reflect the new belief. In all of the apostle Paul's missionary trips, he never pleaded with pagans to change their outward behavior. Rather, he sought to convince them regarding the identity of Jesus Christ as God. Why? Because, behavior is merely a symptomatic reflection of our view of God. This is true for the non-Christian and the Christian alike. If the behavior is wrong, we should take a close look at the underlying God-concept. Attempting to correct wrong behavior while ignoring a person's underlying view of God is short-sighted and ultimately destined to fail. It is simply another form of behavior modification.

It is time for many of us to exchange our sword for a fishing pole.

In Luke 19:10, following His encounter with a *hated* tax collector named Zacchaeus, Jesus was very clear that He came to "seek and to save what was lost." Why should our agenda be any different? Jesus said, "Follow me, and I will make you fishers of men" (Matthew 4:19). Are we fishing, or are we scaring the fish away? We are called to be messengers effectively extending God's heart of love and forgiveness to a hurting world, not merely "Teachers of the Law." It is time for many of us to exchange our sword for a fishing pole.

In the following chapters we will explore some ways in which our words may become more relevant to the culture surrounding us.

Review Questions

1. Cite a time in your life when you have drawn your emotional and rhetorical "sword" in an effort to judge or repudiate the behavior of some in our culture. Cite a time when you took out your "fishing pole" in an effort to reach them. How do you explain the difference in your motivation?

2. What evidence would you cite that shows your heart reflects God's heart for "sinners" in our culture?

3. What national or social issues do you pray about on a regular basis?

4. How bold are you in making God's perspective known to neighbors, coworkers, or civic leaders? What price, if any, have you had to pay for your boldness?

5. To what degree is lack of knowledge or training an issue in your willingness to take a stand for God's perspective in our culture? What kinds of training do you need in order to be more effective?

CHAPTER 3

REFRAMING THE ISSUE

*"Give to Caesar what is Caesar's,
and to God what is God's."*
—*Jesus (Matthew 22:21)*

Great communicators and leaders know that to be effective, they must first develop their message and then stay focused on their message no matter what. This was illustrated in 1994 at the University of Washington in Seattle. That fall term clearly demonstrated the importance and effectiveness of staying on message without deviation.

During the second week of school, Todd, a student, came up to an information table that Campus Crusade for Christ had set up in front of the dorms. His first question was, "Can I sign up for a Bible Study?" The student sitting behind the table, of course, responded affirmatively. His follow-up question came more to the point. "I'm gay. Can I still sign up?" The young woman again responded with an unequivocal, "Yes, we would love for you to join us." That was probably not the answer he expected. Finally, he asked, "Is there anything I would not be allowed to do because of being gay?" Her next response finally gave him what he had wanted all along. As graciously as she knew how, she explained that due to biblical prohibitions he could not hold any position of leadership in ministry as long as he actively engaged in homosexual behavior. His all too familiar parting mantra was, "I'm offended."

The next day, the front page of *The Daily* (the student newspaper) read "Christian group won't allow gay students to be leaders."[25] The following edition featured an editorial entitled "Why is CCC's discrimination condoned by UW?"[26] There was a call to revoke Campus Crusade's charter as an officially recognized student organization. It was a classic setup.

Our response was not to cower but to confront. However, we refused to do so on our opponents' terms. The following week we handed out 10,000 flyers at all the major foot traffic points leading into campus. The flyer never used the words "homosexuality" or "homosexual"; rather, it made reference to "a small, vocal minority." Most students knew who we meant, but we did not want to do anything to distract from our ability to aggressively co-opt and control the rhetorical initiative. We wanted to reframe the issue as "censorship" rather than intolerance. If we had used the word "homosexuality" it would have watered down the focus of our message. We then accused the "small, vocal minority" of being hypocritical, of undermining true diversity, of seeking to ban free speech, and of practicing censorship. The first step was to put them in a defensive posture.

We then ended the front page of the bifold flyer with the question, "What are they afraid you might hear?" This allowed us to segue into our issue: the God of the Bible and Jesus Christ. It also allowed us to wrest control of the rhetorical playing field.

For the next three months, our opponents attacked, calling us homophobes and bigots, while *we strategically ignored their issue*. We countered by accusing them of *censorship*, thereby putting them right back in a defensive posture. We then continued, following up with the question, "What don't they want you to hear?" allowing us to again talk about our issue—God. We wanted to debate cause, not effect. We understood that treating symptoms while ignoring the underlying disease is shortsighted.

For the entire fall semester the militant homosexuals gave us a platform, which we gratefully accepted. However, they finally figured out two things: first, that under no circumstances were we going to be so foolish as to talk about their agenda—homosexual behavior; and second, *every* time they attacked they were going to be accused of censorship. The strategy kept them in an untenable defensive posture, while simultaneously giving us the opportunity to talk about our issue—Jesus Christ.

Finally, in December, they went away with one final, frustrated whimper from the opinion editor of *The Daily*, a self-acknowledged homosexual. They realized they were doing themselves no favors. Not only were they expending a lot of effort and not making any headway, they were actually losing ground. We were hammering them about censorship while ignoring the homosexual issue. And by talking about Jesus Christ, we were actually undermining their position since a person cannot reasonably embrace the God of the Bible while engaging in behavior that the Bible deems immoral.

Allow me to parenthetically touch on a relevant issue at this point. Some religious people say that the God of the Bible does not condemn homosexual behavior despite the fact that every clear biblical reference to such conduct is, *without exception*, negative. In the entire Bible, there is *not even one* clear statement regarding homosexual behavior that is positive. Not one! (If every statement I make about spinach is negative, then an intelligent person will soon come to the conclusion that I do not like spinach.) In light of this, the burden of proof is heavy indeed upon those who try to assert that the Bible condones homosexual behavior in any way, shape or form. My challenge to such individuals is to show me just one ***clear*** statement about any form of homosexual behavior that the God of the Bible speaks of in a positive manner. Just one. If they can I will gladly reconsider my position.

Truth is always the first casualty whenever we start with what we want rather than with who God is.

If we adapt Aldous Huxley's statement (which I referred to in Chapter One) to this context I believe it would read something like this, "The homosexual who finds that the Bible does not censure homosexual behavior is not concerned exclusively with a problem in theology. He is also concerned to prove that there is no valid reason why he personally should not do as he wants."[ii] Once again we see that Truth is always the first casualty whenever we start with what we want rather than with who God is.

The strategy we used at the University of Washington is not new. In Matthew chapter 22, the Pharisees came to Jesus and asked Him if it was lawful to pay taxes to Caesar. They were

---

[ii] So that you do not have to flip back to chapter 1, here is Aldous Huxley's statement once again. "The philosopher who finds no meaning in the world is not concerned exclusively with a problem in metaphysics. He is also concerned to prove that there is no valid reason why he personally should not do as he wants."

trying to set Him up just as the "inquiring" university student had done to us. If Jesus said, "No," He would risk arousing the ire of the Roman ruling establishment. If He said, "Yes," the masses, which passionately hated their foreign overlords, might turn against Him. Therefore, instead of answering the question, Jesus accused His opponents of being "hypocrites," thereby attacking their credibility in an area in which they were vulnerable and putting them on the defensive. (This is the same tactic we used at the University of Washington by legitimately accusing our opposition of censorship and hypocrisy.)

When God becomes the central issue, debates about secondary matters often take care of themselves and even go away.

Jesus then followed up by reframing the question: Since the money the Jews used bore the image of Caesar, was it not his? If so, was it right to withhold from Caesar what was rightfully his? But Jesus did not leave the discussion there—His real goal was not to settle an issue about money, but to point people to God. Therefore, immediately after telling them, "Give to Caesar what is Caesar's," He added, "and to God what is God's" (Matthew 22:21). He did not just address the issue at hand—man's obligation to the state. Rather, He used the opportunity to springboard into the greater issue of man's obligation to God. In the process He also exposed the Pharisees' hypocrisy. They weren't concerned about whether or not they should pay taxes (any more than the inquiring college student was actually interested in leading one of our Bible studies). The Pharisees' goal was to maintain their own power by discrediting someone they viewed as a threat. But when Jesus took the initiative and reframed the terms of the debate, the same thing occurred as ultimately happened at the University of Washington: "they left and went away" (v. 22). When God becomes the central issue, debates about secondary matters often take care of themselves and even go away.

Matthew chapter 21 records how the religious leaders came to Jesus seeking to corner Him by inquiring about the source of His authority. They hoped to either trap Him into claiming equality with God so they could stone Him, or rhetorically undermine the basis of His authority. However, Jesus made it clear that if they wanted Him to answer their question, they would first have to answer a question for Him regarding the source of authority of John the Baptist: was it God or man? Whichever way they answered His question, they were going to look bad. Jesus put them in a lose/lose situation while making God the pivotal issue in the debate about the source of legitimate authority. Again, Jesus had turned the rhetorical tables, and made God the issue.

In John chapter 8, when the woman caught in adultery was brought to Jesus, the Jewish religious leaders asked if she should be stoned to death according to the Law of Moses. Again, they were trying to trap Jesus. If He did not uphold the Law, they would have a basis for bringing charges against Him. If He did uphold the letter of the Law, He would likely alienate those to whom He was trying to communicate—the masses. So, instead of directly answering the question, He broadened the terms of the debate in order to uphold the Law, put the religious leaders in a defensive posture, save the woman from stoning, and give her an opportunity to leave her life of sin. His well-known response was, "If any one of you is without sin, let him be the first to throw a stone at her" (John 8:7). The first person to throw a stone would therefore be claiming to be sinless, the same thing to a Jew as claiming equality with God—a crime punishable by stoning. Jesus effectively used his opponents' view of God to take control of the situation.

In each case, rather than answering the question, Jesus wrested control of the debate by hijacking the question as a platform for His agenda. Much like an able politician or debater, He moved from defense to offense by always redefining the rhetorical playing field, thereby outflanking the opposition. In essence, Jesus hijacked the question. When confronted by those who tried to trap Him, He consistently and skillfully reframed the question so as to stay on message, thereby pointing people to His Father. We should learn how to do likewise and attempt to do no less.

These examples illustrate the principle of how we may transcend almost any issue, including homosexual behavior or abortion, ultimately making the God of the Bible the focus of the debate, allowing us to stay on offense and control the rhetorical playing field.

In today's American culture, we must first recognize that the amoral forces of "tolerance" are currently in the driver's seat, which means those of us who disagree with them are, by default, on the defense. The war in Vietnam painfully reminded us as a nation that a great defense can rarely do more than delay defeat.

On the other hand, Bill Clinton consistently demonstrated that the best defense is actually a tireless "take no prisoners" offense. For instance, instead of reacting to the phrase "family values," he and his adminstration hijacked the term by redefining "family" from a father, mother, and their children to pretty much whatever the individual wanted it to be. Instead of honestly answering questions under oath before a grand jury about his affair with Monica Lewinski, he disingenuously reframed in a misleading way by parsing the meaning of "is" when he said, "It depends on what that meaning of the word 'is' is." Distract. Divert. Spin. Counter-charge. He always found a way to duck and then move back onto the offense—to stay on message. Although he lacked any vestige of integrity, he was masterful with rhetoric. Only rarely did he directly answer charges leveled at him. He understood the well-worn political adage, "I don't want my opponent to admit anything, I just want him to deny it."

Those who want to remove God from our culture understand that if they can control the terms of the debate keeping us on defense, they can also control the outcome.

Bill Clinton understood that in order to win, he had to be on offense making the charges, not trying to defend himself against them. Likewise, those who want to remove God from

RATHER THAN
ANSWERING THE
QUESTION, JESUS
WRESTED CONTROL
OF THE DEBATE
BY HIJACKING
THE QUESTION AS
A PLATFORM FOR
HIS AGENDA.

our culture understand that if they can control the *terms* of the debate keeping us on defense, they can also control the outcome. If we are to win, we must reframe the entire issue in a manner that allows us to move back onto the offense—to stay on message.

Therefore, if our rhetorical response is merely to condemn a symptomatic issue such as homosexual behavior, abortion, racism, or pornography as morally reprehensible (which they are), we will lose (i.e., the behavior will continue, or other symptomatic behavior will replace it). In much of our culture, condemning immoral behavior is deemed intolerant (opposition to racism being the one notable exception—at least for now). And if we come across as intolerant, we lose much of our ability to communicate to a large segment of our culture, which is exactly what the opposition wants. But here is the real bottom line: each time we defensively react to their issue, they are able to further marginalize us in the eyes of the broad culture, and worse, get us off message. It is that simple—and that profound.

Matthew 13:24–30 records the story Jesus told of a farmer who discovered that someone had planted weeds in his wheat field. He instructed his employees to let the weeds grow up with the wheat until harvest time, so that uprooting the intertwined weeds would not damage the wheat. Likewise, God does not ask us to pull weeds in His wheat field; rather we are instructed to nurture, water, and fertilize His crop until the time when He harvests it.

In this regard, I believe that when Jesus said, "Do not judge, or you too will be judged," He was making more than just a moral proclamation. He was also making a statement containing the seeds of a powerful strategy, because He knew that the most powerful force in the universe is love, not hate, nor its cousin, condemnation. In the words of Martin Luther King, Jr., "Darkness cannot drive out darkness; only light can do that. Hate cannot drive out hate; only love can do that."[27] Jesus demonstrated this when he laid down His life for us out of love; He did not come to condemn us, even though the basis for condemnation is very real. Therefore, God Himself, the author of love, is the logical starting point in changing our culture.

The goal is to reestablish the critical connection in people's minds between God and morality

---

In order to make God the starting point, we must first establish a clear link in the minds of our fellow citizens between their view of God and their position on any given moral issue. Let me re-emphasize I am not talking about addressing moral content, which comes later in the process. Rather, the goal is to reestablish the critical connection in people's minds between God and morality. In the minds of many Americans, there is currently a disconnect (a firewall) between belief in God and their position on many moral issues due to the pervasive influence of moral relativism. For instance, in modern society we often hear the question, "How does that make you feel?" as though my feelings are the most important consideration. Wherever this question pops up in regard to a moral issue, we should always reframe with "How do you think that makes God feel?" moving the focus from self to God. We must intentionally help reconnect the intellectual disconnect. In this process, the opposition unintentionally gives us a platform to advance our agenda, similar to what occurred at the University of Washington.

The operating premise here is summed up in the often-heard political response, "That's a good question, but I think the real issue is…" In other words, do not answer the question asked; rather, view the question as an opportunity to talk about our issue—the God of the Bible. As we saw earlier in this chapter, Jesus effectively used this strategy to His advantage on many occasions. Initially, we must strategically ignore the "good question" of the moral rightness or wrongness of a given matter and move immediately to the "critical question" of the existence and identity of God, who is the basis of morality itself. Without God, morality is little more than a fairy tale on the same level as Santa Claus and the Easter bunny

This tactic is critical for several reasons:

- First, the time is ripe. On September 11, 2001, the entire playing field shifted in our favor. Since that day, God has been far more welcome in the public square than He has been in decades. Even U.S. Senator Joseph Lieberman said in a speech at Notre Dame, "We as a nation must strengthen our moral foundation because so many of the social problems…are at their heart moral problems." A few moments later he closed the loop by saying, "I believe that we are still struggling to regain our moral balance, in part because we are struggling to regain our spiritual balance."[28]

- Second, it allows us to move the terms of the debate away from issues over which we have limited control, toward an issue that we can frame and direct. The opposition will still attack. In fact, they may initially react with an intensity we rarely see. However, the key difference is that we will be able to begin taking territory rather than continuing to lose it. This does not mean that we will necessarily convince our opponents, but we will be better positioned to influence the thinking of the masses who are not already committed to an anti-God ideology.

- Third, according to pollster George Barna, 85 percent of Americans consider themselves "Christian," Of these, 8 percent are evangelicals, 33 percent are born-again non-evangelicals, and 44 percent are "notional Christians." (The latter are those who consider themselves to be Christian, but do not embrace core Bible doctrines.[29]) This means we will tend to have an audience predisposed to our point of view if we choose our words wisely. Our challenge is to always relate the debate back to the God of the Bible.

- Fourth, once we establish linkage in people's minds between God and a given moral issue, it will be an easy matter to establish the same link between God and any other moral issue. Once our foot is in the door, it is easy to begin opening it even wider.

- Fifth, it enables us to make the existence and identity of God the central issue we must debate as a nation. Once this occurs, we are in the driver's seat. At that point the principles of social change will work in our favor *if we stay on message*. We have the opportunity to shift the debate from sexual preference, death with dignity, or "choice" to the underlying question, "Who is God?"

- Sixth, God is the underlying watershed issue.

Let me once again reemphasize, our view of God will determine our belief system as individuals and as a society. If we fail to make the God of the Bible the issue, we will most certainly and inevitably fail to reestablish the moral foundation of the nation. Not only is God the central issue, but "God" is the only issue (when properly framed) that can consistently enable us to maintain control of the rhetorical playing field. Is it therefore any wonder that the opposition strives with such passion to censor religious speech in the public square—especially in education?

Chapter 1 Review Questions

1. How comfortable are you in the "offensive" role—taking the debate to our opponents rather than just defending yourself against the opponents' charges?

2. How can Christians balance aggressiveness and love? Are the two compatible or mutually exclusive? When does aggressiveness cross the line into carnality?

3. How would you evaluate your temperament—pro-active (offense) or compliant (defense)? If you are not naturally aggressive, how willing are you to take on that role when necessary in order to make God the issue?

4. When Jesus demonstrated aggressive behavior in words and action (such as driving the money-changers out of the temple), was He doing something unique to Himself or setting an example for all of His followers? Why?

5. Statistically speaking, why should it not be difficult to reframe the rhetorical debate about God in America with the general population? If the majority of Americans claim to believe in God, why isn't God found throughout the public square in our culture?

CHAPTER 4

THE SEVEN RULES OF SOCIAL CHANGE

"A wise man has great power,
and a man of knowledge increases strength."
—King Solomon of Israel (Proverbs 24:5)

Any substantive change in society comes with a price tag. Societies, like the people who compose them, resist change, and often make agents of change pay dearly for disrupting the status quo. However, there are some historical rules of engagement which if properly understood and followed will exponentially increase our chances of changing any culture. We can ignore them, but only to the detriment of our cause. Many of them are common sense; others do not seem to be quite so common. Some of them we have already discussed, but the goal of this chapter is to place them in context to show how they work together. Understanding and applying these principles can produce powerful change. As the familiar saying goes, *knowledge is power.*

RULE #1: NEVER, NEVER, NEVER GIVE IN!
WHAT PRICE ARE YOU WILLING TO PAY?

In 1941, during the dark, foreboding days of World War II, Winston Churchill, the prime minister of Great Britain, addressed his alma mater, the Harrow School. Some of his most memorable words come in the midst of this oratory: "Never give in. Never give in. Never, never, never, never—in nothing, great or small, large or petty—never give in...."[30] Winston Churchill understood the depth of commitment it takes to change the course of history.

Only a relative handful of people are required to move the thinking of the broader culture but that group must be highly committed to its cause. They must be willing to sacrifice everything. This seems to be what history unmistakably indicates.

In 1903, at a meeting of the Russian Social Democratic Labor Party, the qualifications for membership were debated. One man, Vladimir Lenin, vehemently demanded nothing less than total and complete commitment to the Communist cause for life. Seventeen men joined with him. Fourteen years later, when they seized power in the Soviet Union—a nation of 150 million people—there were still only four thousand members of the Communist Party. A handful of people took over one of the most powerful nations on earth, and then proceeded to spread their humanist ideology to the rest of the world through propaganda and military force.[31]

Only a relative handful of people are required to move the thinking of the broader culture

---

A number of years ago, Billy Graham shared a letter that an American college student had written to his fiancée, explaining why he was breaking off their engagement. Following is an excerpt of that letter:

We communists have a high casualty rate. We live in virtual poverty, and turn back every penny we make to the Party above what is absolutely necessary to keep us alive. We communists don't have the time or the money for movies, concerts, or T-bone steaks or decent homes or new cars. I am in dead earnest. Communism is my life, my business, my religion, my sweetheart, my wife, my mistress, my bread and meat. I work at it in the daytime and dream about it at night. Its hold on me grows, not lessens, as time goes by. Therefore, I cannot carry on a friendship, a love affair, or even a conversation without relating to this force which both drives and guides my life. I've already been in jail because of my ideas and if necessary I am ready to go before a firing squad.

Our Founding Fathers understood this principle. All fifty-six of the men who signed the Declaration of Independence knew that they might well die a traitor's death. Nine of their rank did die during the Revolutionary War. Five others were captured and tortured by the British. Twelve lost their homes; seventeen lost their fortunes; two lost their sons. Despite all this, not a single one defected. Not a single man failed to honor his pledge as stated in the final sentence of the Declaration of Independence: "For the support of this declaration, with a firm reliance on the protection of Divine Providence, we mutually pledge to each other our lives, our fortunes, and our sacred honor." In the end, despite the odds, they triumphed.

William Wilberforce, a member of the House of Parliament

around the turn of the 19th century, persisted for twenty years before seeing the slave trade ended in the British Empire. A small group of influential men known as the Clapham Sect did their part in assisting him. During most of those years his peers in Parliament mercilessly ridiculed him. But in the end he triumphed, standing on the shoulders of the members of the Clapham Sect who had joined with him heart and soul.

Twenty years ago, a young Christian couple decided to tell the people of their nation about Jesus. They were from an Asian country that was closed to the message of God's Son, where any type of proselytizing would result in imprisonment or death. At that time there were approximately five hundred known Christians in the country.

Today, the gospel of Jesus Christ has been heard throughout that country through the persistence and tenacity of that one couple who totally committed themselves to following Jesus (enduring imprisonment along the way). As a result, approximately twenty-five percent of that nation's citizens now follow the God of the Bible. Although there are still very real challenges for those who truly follow Jesus, the official policy of that government has changed to one of religious toleration. That nation has forever been changed, and is continuing to change because of two people who were willing to pay the ultimate price.

In 1951, an ambitious young California businessman wrote out a contract with God, agreeing to go anywhere and do anything God asked. And he meant it. He left himself no escape clauses—no wiggle room. And then he proceeded to live out his agreement. He started going to the local university campus to speak to students about Jesus. He recruited others to go with him. Five years later he sold his businesses to devote all of his time to evangelism and discipleship. For over fifty years he never looked back. He never wavered.

What he left in his wake was a movement of like-minded individuals who have touched over six billion people in virtually every corner of the world. Today, over 25,000 full-time and approximately 250,000 trained volunteer staff seek to tell everyone who will listen about the Good News of Jesus Christ in just about every country on the face of the earth. The name of the movement is Campus Crusade for Christ, and the name of the man was Bill Bright. God can do great things through anyone who will wholeheartedly commit to Him without reservation.

All but one of Jesus' disciples died as martyrs (excluding Judas the traitor, of course). The other, John, was burned alive in oil by the Romans and then exiled to the island of Patmos. The apostle Paul received thirty-nine lashes on five occasions. He was beaten with rods three times, stoned once, and shipwrecked three times (2 Corinthians 6:3-10, 11:16-29). But he, as well as all the other apostles, persevered through overwhelming obstacles. Empowered by the Spirit of God, they turned the Roman Empire upside down.

This is the first principle of social change: there must be a handful who are willing to give everything for the cause—who are willing to persevere no matter the personal cost. Like Vladimir Lenin, they must say, "Nothing but total and complete commitment!" Along with Winston Churchill, they must say, "Never, never, never give in!" Like the apostle Paul, they must believe in their hearts that, "to live is Christ and to die is gain."[32] Like Bill Bright, they must make an irrevocable contract with God.

RULE #2: KEEP YOUR EYES ON THE NORTH STAR.

IS YOUR GOAL CLEAR?

Over the centuries, ships in the northern hemisphere navigated by the North Star. It was a set point by which they could determine their position on the map. Without it, nighttime navigation would have been virtually impossible.

Likewise, we all need a set point by which to navigate. If we want to bring about change, we need to be clear in our own minds, not only what needs to be changed, but what the end result should look like. We need to determine our core agenda and make every decision in light of it.

During President Clinton's administration I routinely heard "Bill Clinton's only goal is Bill Clinton." Baloney! He may well have had a massive ego, but he also had a very definite agenda. It was an object that dwarfed everything he gave away in payment.

Had he not had a fatal character flaw when it came to personal integrity and sexual conduct, he probably would have accomplished his goal. When it came to his personal life, he did not make decisions in light of his core agenda—and he paid dearly for it. Although he beat the Republicans over "Monicagate" (he was impeached but not removed from office), he had to spend so much personal political capital in that battle that he never fully recovered. He became a laughingstock across America among conservatives, moderates, and even many liberals. His sexual conduct became the brunt of jokes on radio and late-night television. It got so bad that Al Gore, while seeking to become the Democratic nominee for President, felt obliged to lay a major televised smooch on his wife during the Democratic National Convention in order to send a clear message to the American people that he was not a philanderer like Clinton. And yet many in the media say that character does not matter in politics today.

Bill Clinton's agenda was the courts. He wanted to fill the courts with secular revisionist jurists[33] so that America could be reshaped in his image over the next twenty years by circumventing the cantankerous and independent-minded legislative process. Legislators are accountable to the people of their districts and states. Judges at the Federal level are largely accountable to no one apart from other judges. Therefore if the courts become stacked with secular revisionist judges, there really is no accountability, and rampant wholesale change can proceed without real impediment.

Needless to say, Clinton did not complete his agenda. Because the Republican-controlled Senate dragged its feet on confirmations, it became clear to Mr. Clinton by the end of his first term in the White House that in order to complete the process he would have to put his hand-picked successor into office in order to finish the job. That man was Al Gore whose bid for the White House failed by the narrowest margin in history.

The point is this: Bill Clinton had an agenda toward which he moved the nation as far as he could. Anything that did not directly contribute to that agenda became fodder for building the political capital he needed to push through his primary agenda. Bill Clinton knew what he wanted and made all of his political (but foolishly, not his personal) decisions in light of it. Though we can be thankful he did not accomplish his agenda in full, we can learn from his example the power of making decisions in light of a single goal.

> We must determine our primary goal and then be willing to give away the rest of the store in order to accomplish it.

In regard to this principle, allow me a personal reflection for a moment. You read in the Foreword to this book of my father's desire to chain himself to the Supreme Court until Roe v. Wade was overturned. What you didn't read is that it was more than my mother's hand that restrained my father. For nearly half a century my father constrained himself by choice to follow the path and complete the agenda that God gave Him: fulfilling the Great Commission of Jesus Christ. As badly as he might have wanted to enter other venues, and as capable as he would have been if he had, he stayed focused on his primary agenda and subordinated everything else in life to it. He is a living example of the fruit that is born from setting an agenda and remaining committed to it.

During my 20's I worked as an aide to U.S. Senator William Armstrong from Colorado. One of the things I greatly admired about him was his ability to say "No" to many good things in order to say "Yes" to those few critical things that best enabled him to move his agenda forward. Without that ability, he never would have achieved much of anything.

Likewise, we must determine our primary goal and then be willing to give away the rest of the store in order to accomplish it. This will mean saying "No" to many worthy causes. We cannot win every battle, and, in fact, we should not try to win every battle. But if we strategically chose our battles with great care in light of our core agenda, our North Star, we can win the war.

RULE #3: KNOW YOUR AREOPAGUS
WHO IS YOUR AUDIENCE?

Acts chapter 17 tells the story of the apostle Paul's experience in Athens. We learn that when he arrived he was "distressed" by all the idols. However, instead of reacting and condemning idol worship he sized up his audience and tailored his message accordingly. Walking through the streets of the city he noticed an altar "TO AN UNKNOWN GOD."[34] Rather than reacting, he used this as a springboard to explain to the Areopagus (the leaders of Athens) who the Creator God really is. He even complimented them on being religious and quoted their own Greek poets in an effort to establish common ground on which to build the case for Jesus.

Paul did three very wise things. First, he determined who his audience was. They were Greeks, not Jews. They were polytheists, not monotheists. Second, he framed his message seeking common ground as a starting point, so he could help his audience better understand and accept his message. Even though he was deeply offended by idolatry, he did not start off by condemning them for it. Rather, he chose to begin with images and concepts to which they could relate. Third, although he was extremely creative and very out-of-the-box in how he framed his message (note that he did not even use the name of

Jesus, probably because the name itself would have been meaningless to the Greeks), he did not water down the essence or the person of the gospel. He was clear. He gave his audience an unmistakable choice.

In determining your audience, two factors are important: the receptivity of a particular audience, and their potential ability to exert influence.

The Areopagus principle is very straightforward: determine who your audience is and tailor your words accordingly. This is standard practice in most Christian missions around the globe: we learn a culture's language and customs, then we translate the gospel into terms they can understand. This same principle applies even in the nearby cultures of unchurched America. However, in determining your audience, two factors are important: the receptivity of a particular audience, and their potential ability to exert influence.

Paul always began his preaching at the local Jewish synagogue (if there was one) whenever he entered a new town. The reason was simple: he was most likely to find a receptive audience there for his message due to the large amount of shared belief (common ground). This is generally how Paul got the "camel's nose under the edge of the tent" in a city. Once he had established a base of converts, he could then begin to expand it in any given community—a simple but smart strategy.

Similarly, at the outset of a political campaign, skilled

politicians rarely expend energy trying to "convert" those who are highly committed to another ideology. Instead, they first try to identify, solidify, and energize those who most closely share their beliefs. This fortifies their "base." Next, the skilled politician tries to frame a message that would appeal to those who lean in his direction. Finally, he targets those who are not highly committed to either side. These "swing votes" usually determine the outcome of the election.

As I mentioned in Chapter 3, 85 percent of Americans consider themselves Christian, meaning that we have rhetorical common ground with 85 percent of Americans. However, we should begin with the evangelical 8 percent (the most logical base for our "God of the Bible" message), expand to the "born-again non-evangelical" 33 percent (those who tend to lean toward accepting our message), and then expand to the remaining "notional" 44 percent (those who could probably go either way). It is a logical progression and an effective strategy.

We should also try to target centers of influence wherever possible. This can be a geographical place, person, or institution. This is why Paul went to the Areopagus, even though he shared minimal common ground with them. Paul consistently went to the influential cities of his day—centers of political, economic, religious, and academic influence. This was clearly deliberate on his part. For instance, Athens was an academic center. Ephesus was a religious and economic hub. Corinth was a resort town where many of the "rich and famous" lived. Rome was the political and economic center of the empire. (Although he went there in chains, he had long made it clear that getting there was one of his goals.) In Acts 9:15, God told Ananias regarding

Paul, "This man is my chosen instrument to carry my name before the Gentiles *and their kings* and before the people of Israel" (emphasis added). Among other things, God specifically tasked Paul with telling the "kings" of his day about Jesus. We should be just as strategic in planning how we may reach the influencers of our day to whom God gives us access.

It is for this reason that Campus Crusade for Christ often focuses on reaching centers of influence on a college campus or in a city, state, or nation. If we reach the influencers, they can help us reach everyone else—either from up front or behind the scenes. Sometimes influential individuals or groups take a high-profile role. Other times they quietly open doors without much fanfare. Each situation is different, but the principle remains.

In order to succeed, we must be intentional in determining our audience—both those who are most likely to be open to accepting our message and those who can most effectively help us disseminate our message.

Of course, after we determine our audience, we must tailor our message accordingly. We speak differently to an adult than to a child. My vocabulary when conversing with a philosophy professor is quite different than when I talk with my son's kindergarten teacher. Speaking in a fraternity house is much different than speaking in church on Sunday. The Areopagus is a world apart from a synagogue. Even if the core message is identical, the words are very different—adapted to the particular audience.

The message should be framed from the outset to capture the rhetorical upper hand, often referred to as achieving the "perceived" moral high ground. This is critical to the process.

If a cause cannot capture the rhetorical offense, it can never win.

If a cause cannot capture the rhetorical offense, it can never win. This explains in large measure why we continue to lose ground on the issues of abortion ("choice") and homosexual behavior ("tolerance") within the cultural context. If, on the other hand, we can shift the bulk of the debate to discussing who God is, and resist the temptation to go back on the defense by debating cultural symptoms, it will greatly increase our chances of changing the culture itself.

When I was eighteen years old, I traveled with my parents to the former Soviet Union for a couple weeks. While we were there, our Russian guide told us a joke about a dual track meet between the United States and the Soviet Union which the Americans won. However, the headline the next day in the Russian newspaper read, "Soviets come in second, Americans next to last." Though fictitious, the story illustrates how perspective (spin) is critical.

The perspective we present affects perception, and perception has power to create change. In politics, many even go so far as to say, "Perception is everything." That is why politicians expend so much energy trying to get just the right "spin." They understand that if you can change a person's perception, then you can also change his beliefs, values, views, and behavior.

About ten years ago while I was in the Philippines, I read in the local newspaper that Philippine President Aquino during her trip to the U.S. had met with the Vice President of the United

States at a military installation (the article conveniently failed to mention which military installation). The paper was very critical of her for this, because at the time many Philippine activists were trying to oust the U.S. from its military bases in the Philippines. Upon reading the article, I started chuckling. I happened to know which military installation was being referenced—the U.S. Naval Observatory, on the grounds of which is the official residence of the Vice President of the United States. One key detail can make a huge difference.

About a year after I joined the staff of Campus Crusade for Christ, I moved to Seattle to work with our ministry team at the University of Washington. Several times people said to me with sympathy in their voice that the Northwest was the most "un-churched" part of the country. The clear implication was that the people there were unresponsive to the gospel. How wrong they were. I soon realized that students in the Northwest were very open to the gospel, but I also quickly learned that, like the apostle Paul, I could not use "churchy" words and had to adapt my presentation accordingly.

In the seven years I was there I spoke to many fraternity pledge classes. With only two exceptions, every time I spoke, over half of the young men present indicated that they would like to know more about how to know God personally. In framing my message, I always began with their felt need and then used that as a springboard into their real need (a relationship with God). For instance, I would go in to talk about "Leadership" and then transition to the greatest Leader who ever lived—Jesus Christ. Or I would talk about "Brotherhood," and then introduce them to the one Person who best modeled what a true brother was—

Jesus Christ (He gave up His life for His friends). The point was always to help them grasp that Jesus Christ was relevant to their lives today. I was a messenger attempting to deliver the message to the best of my ability, and therefore I worked hard to tailor it to my audience.

One of the international ministries of Campus Crusade for Christ is called "Crossroads." It uses the issue of AIDS to bring the message of Jesus Christ to the people of countries devastated by the epidemic. It is a program designed for schools to use in educating young people about AIDS and how they can protect themselves by changing their behavior. In the process, we present Jesus as the one who can empower them to make these behavioral changes in their lives. We start from their felt need (avoiding AIDS) and show how it relates to their real everyday need for God.

Jesus consistently did this. He almost always began with stories to which His audience could relate. He gave them something they could readily understand, and then rhetorically moved them to where He wanted them to go. Most of Jesus' teaching followed this pattern. He not only knew His message—He knew His audience.

With the woman at the well, He spoke first of water because they were at a well (John 4:4–42). With the hated tax collector, He first granted social acceptance by welcoming the opportunity to eat a meal with him (Luke 19:2). With the theologian Nicodemus, He raised the most profound theological issue: "You must be born again" (John 3:1–21). With the woman caught in adultery, He first provided for her physical security by shaming her accusers into leaving (John 8:3–11). Jesus always tailored His words to His audience.

Someone has said that God is like an elevator operator: He meets you at your level and takes you where you need to go. He passionately loves you as you are, but He loves you so much that He is not willing to let you stay there.

Recently, I met with several leaders of a Christian denomination. They were seeking to craft a document justifying the actions they were taking in a certain city where they had received a great deal of negative feedback for their evangelistic efforts. However, they were attempting to write the document to communicate with both the churched and unchurched at the same time—a near impossible task. The initial document sounded like it was written for theologians, full of "churchy" language, but definitely not for the "Average Joe." Had they published it in that form they would have been "tarred and feathered" in the secular press—and it would have been their own fault. Fortunately, after further discussion, they wisely gave it to some writers who had a good understanding of how to communicate with a secular audience. The final document sounded quite different than the original, even though it basically said the same thing.

George W. Bush, in his response to the Muslim terrorists, said that we would pursue an aggressive "crusade" against them. To the average American, the word "crusade" is rather innocuous. But to an Arab Muslim whose ancestors were the focus of the "Crusades" almost a thousand years ago, it is just as offensive (even more so, if that is possible) as derogatory racial slurs and epithets are to ethnic minorities in America. To an Arab Muslim, pouring gasoline on a fire is no less inflammatory. Fortunately, President Bush learned quickly and made that mistake only once. Had he done it again, even our closest allies in the Arab world might not have stood with us. The words we use will greatly influence how our audience responds.

In order for our message to be understood, we must understand who our listeners are, how they think, and how they speak. In this regard, how we say something is almost as important as what we say. As I mentioned in Chapter 2, words like "grace," "salvation," "born again," "sinner," and even "Christian" are often misunderstood by a secular audience. Although these words are very important to all followers of Jesus, our goal should always be to communicate the concepts that the words represent. There is no magic in the words themselves. But just like missionaries in foreign cultures, we too should adopt a cross-cultural mindset. Although like the apostle Paul we must never compromise our message. We desperately need to become experts at communicating the gospel using words that our audience already understands.

RULE #4: REFRAME! REFRAME! REFRAME!
NEVER FEEL OBLIGATED TO ANSWER THE QUESTION

People who invest in real estate know that the three most important criteria are: "Location. Location. Location." Similarly, anyone who has been an effective agent for change within culture knows the three most critical elements to bringing about change in the way people think are: "Reframe! Reframe! Reframe!"

According to Webster's Dictionary, reframe means "to frame again." That is exactly the point. No matter how someone else frames an issue, I always reframe my rhetoric in a manner that allows me to communicate my agenda in the most effective way possible. What this requires is a commitment to never react and always stay on message no matter the rhetorical curve balls that come your way trying to knock you off message and distract you from your goal.

Following one of our rhetorical skirmishes at the University of Washington, my wife received a plaque from some friends. It had a picture of a skier slicing through the water kicking up a wall of spray. The picture was entitled, "Sometimes, in order to stay the course, you have to make waves." I often think of that picture when I am tempted to take the route of least resistance.

Staying on message, staying the course, requires being intentional. It takes work, thought, and training. And often it takes courage. But it never "just happens" because it requires us to constantly reframe our message in order to stay on course. It's all about consistently moving from defense to offense. Like life itself, it is a fluid process. Although a good defense is important, you cannot win unless you intentionally move onto offense.

For instance, if someone approaches you and says, "I'm offended that you prayed in the name of Jesus," your first natural response might be to apologize for having given offense. However, if you have given it thought ahead of time you might respond in the following manner: "I'm offended you would try to censor the content of my speech. Isn't that a rather un-American thing to do? And besides, what do you have against Jesus?" In 28 words, you have put your prosecutor in a defensive position, and you are now back on message, in control of the rhetorical playing field, talking about God. This is exactly what the apostles did routinely, such as Peter's response to the Sanhedrin's intimidating threats: "Judge for yourselves whether it is right in God's sight to obey you rather than God."[35] He reframed the issue from obeying the Sanhedrin to obeying God. It never even seemed to cross his mind to apologize for making Jesus the issue.

If we cannot stay on the offense, we cannot win. A great defense, though important, will not move us forward. The entire process can be summed up in four words: Never react—always reframe! Never, never, never answer the question unless it allows you to take the conversation where it needs to go!

As I illustrated in Chapter 3, Jesus never accepted His opponent's terms of debate. He always reframed the issue so that He could make His point. Once we allow the opposition to frame the question, we are on the defense. In the real world this makes it virtually impossible to succeed. In order to move back onto offense, we must reframe the entire question; we must redefine the rhetorical playing field.

I always keep in mind what I call the "3 R's of Social Change." In any given situation we can *Rollover, React or Reframe.* In a nutshell, when we rollover, we choose to do or say nothing. When we react we go on defense trying to stop the opposition from accomplishing its goal. When we reframe we go on offense which forces the opposition to try to stop us.

Choosing to *Rollover,* or to duck, can be a cop out because we just do not want the hassle. This is often the reason we tend to rollover. However there are many times when choosing to rollover can be strategically smart. This is what we mean when we say that we must choose our battles wisely. If I try to engage on every front, I am not likely to do well on any front. I become

The 3 R's of Social Change:

Rollover

React

Reframe

spread too thin. Furthermore, I should try to engage in the battles where I have the best chance of success.

During the Senate confirmation hearings for Justice Anthony Scalia, the Republicans knew they were going to win his confirmation to the Supreme Court. However, they took the opportunity to bait *People for the American Way* into a fight over his confirmation. The net result was the GOP won while *People for the America Way* wasted $5 million on an engagement they never had a reasonable chance of winning. They should have saved their ammunition for another day. They should have chosen to rollover.

On the other hand, I remember when a Christian group on a college campus in the South ran a set of four ads in the student newspaper featuring former homosexuals. Each ad told an individual's story about how he or she became involved in homosexual behavior. Then the individuals related how a personal relationship with Jesus Christ had so radically changed who they were that they no longer craved the homosexual experience. This of course created an uproar in the homosexual community on that campus. Unfortunately, the leader of the Christian group was inadequately trained to effectively manage the controversy. He publicly apologized a few days later for running the ads, instead of turning the tables and legitimately accusing his attackers of hypocrisy and of censoring the speech of people whose personal experience happened to be different than their own. He therefore allowed the homosexual community to hijack the agenda, making the issue "homophobia" rather than Jesus Christ. In effect, he chose to rollover when he could have easily gone on offense, seizing control of the debate and making Jesus the issue.

The second "R" of social change is choosing to *React*. This, by definition, is a defensive posture. Unfortunately, it is often our default position. Reacting is much easier than reframing. Reacting is usually a knee-jerk response. It is always much easier to say "You're wrong!" than to say, "Here is what I think the solution is."

If we focus on trying to suppress all the social ills of our culture, we will only be able slow down the process of decay, never entirely stop it.

However, there does come a time when we need to say "Stop!" We need to say that abortion, racism, homosexual behavior, pornography, abuse of drugs and alcohol are wrong. There is a time to say that sin is sin. There is a time to say "Just quit it!" There is place for the Church to be the conscience of society. That is what the Bible means when it says we are to be "salt." In biblical times, salt was a preservative. It slowed down decay. But please take note that salt never permanently stops decay. It can only slow it down. Likewise, if we focus on trying to suppress all the social ills of our culture, we will only be able slow down the process of decay, never entirely stop it. This is extremely important to understand.

It is fascinating to observe how Jesus always moved from defense to offense as quickly as possible. Even Peter and Paul never told pagans to change their behavior, but rather to change their god.[36] They clearly understood the cause and effect relationship between a person's view of God and their behavior. They understood that the cart can never pull the horse.

> ## Peter and Paul never told pagans to change their behavior, rather they told them to change their god.

Of course, this brings us full circle, back to the third "R" of social change: *Reframe.* It is the only way to move onto offense. It is what Jesus referred to as being "light." Light never tries to stop darkness. Rather, it drives out darkness by its very essence. Light never reacts to darkness, rather darkness always reacts to light. Light is all about offense.

A while ago the city of Orlando was considering an ordinance that would have served to promote homosexual behavior. They held a public hearing where citizens could take a few minutes to state their views in front of the City Council. I decided I would say a few words, but since I believe that homosexual behavior is a symptom, not a cause, I did not want to spend my time trying to suppress a symptom. Attempting to tell people who do not believe in moral absolutes that homosexual behavior is wrong is largely a waste of time. Instead I stood up and stated that as a member of the faith community who believed the Bible was true, my hands were rather tied when it came to supporting homosexual behavior. However, if they could do one thing for me I would be glad to champion their cause for them—prove to me beyond a reasonable doubt that the God of the Bible did not exist, since if God does not exist the Bible cannot be true. Not surprisingly, I had no takers.

Jesus never failed to speak the truth, but He always wisely reframed the question in order to communicate the truth most effectively.

On another occasion, I was teaching a *God is the Issue* seminar in Northern California. I lectured the first hour and then during the second hour answered questions and provided case statements for active hands-on learning. When I opened up the second hour, one of the participants stood up and said he was the head of the gay/lesbian alliance in the local community. After I responded to his numerous questions and made it clear that God loved homosexuals as much as He loved me, the young man said, "You and I really see things pretty much the same way." Having patiently waited for this precise opportunity, I responded by saying, "We couldn't be further apart. You start with your behavior and try to conform God to what you want. I start with God and try to conform my behavior to who God is. Given our radically divergent starting points, we will never come to agreement." My goal was not to debate homosexual behavior, rather it was to change the focus from behavior to God; from symptom to cause.

Jesus never failed to speak the truth, but He always wisely reframed the question to communicate the truth most effectively. As long as we continue to accept the opposition's terms of debate that God is irrelevant to the conversation, there is little hope of ever winning the battle for our culture.

In his book *Rules for Radicals*, Saul Alinsky, a highly effective Marxist political organizer, shrewdly observed, "The real action is in the enemy's reaction…The enemy properly goaded and guided in his reaction will be your major strength."[37] As I mentioned in Chapter 3, in politics I often heard this reflected in the statement, "I don't want to get my opponent to admit anything, I just want to get him to deny it." The point is to force one's opponent into a reactionary defensive mode just like Jesus did. We must always stay on message, and we must force the opposition to react to our agenda if we wish to win.

Never, never, never feel obligated to answer the question!

When we stayed on message at the University of Washington, we got *our* point across and the high-profile opposition eventually evaporated. When William Wilberforce stuck to his guns for twenty years, he finally saw the slave trade outlawed. Because Vladimir Lenin and his associates were totally committed to hammering their message home, they took over one of the largest nations on earth. Because the apostle Paul and his associates preached their message without deviation, despite intense opposition and the very real threat of death, the course of history was changed. When we are willing to carefully craft our words and stay on message no matter the cost, we too can change our world. But it requires focus, wisdom, a disciplined tongue, and perseverance. Never, never, never feel obligated to answer the question! Use the question as a springboard to make God the issue. It can all be summed up in three words: Reframe! Reframe! Reframe!

RULE #5: TURTLES RULE!
HOW DO YOU EAT AN ELEPHANT?

In early childhood we all heard the story about "The Tortoise and the Hare." The hare took off running for the goal line knowing he could easily win the race, but he got distracted along the way. On the other hand, the tortoise plodded along ever so slowly, never stopping, never deviating from the course. We all know who won. The moral of the story was "Slow and steady wins the race." Turtles rule!

But how quickly we forget the lessons learned in childhood. Many Christians want change—which is good. However, they want everything now, and they are unwilling to "compromise," because compromise with the World is "bad." Although this is true, it also reflects a fundamental misunderstanding of the process of bringing about change within a culture.

Let me ask you a few questions. How do you eat an elephant?[38] How do you climb a mountain?[39] If I want to make a million dollars is it wiser to invest in a get-rich-quick-scheme, or should I develop a 30 year investment strategy? How long ago did Jesus give the command to reach the entire world with the message of God's love and plan? Has God completed that process yet or is He still working the plan? Has God compromised? What lesson do we learn from these questions?

I THINK THE PROBLEM MANY CHRISTIANS HAVE IS THEY CONFUSE COMPROMISE WITH PATIENCE.

I think the problem many Christians have is they confuse compromise with patience. Creating further confusion is the well-worn adage that "Politics is the art of compromise." But is it really?

Is it compromise to eat an elephant one bite at time? Or is it necessity? Is it compromise to climb a mountain one step at a time?[39] How else do you get to the top? Is it compromise to take 30 years to make a million dollars? Or is it prudence? Is God's plan for the world behind schedule, or is He right on time? Is politics the art of compromise? Or is it really the process of incremental change? I believe it is the latter. Likewise, the process of changing culture is also incremental. We don't compromise; we simply take it one strategic step at a time, in light of the final objective.

Our goal is to always advance our agenda, thereby continually moving forward and wearing down the opposition. This is not a sprint. It is an endurance race. It requires great patience and perseverance. Like the tortoise, we must keep moving forward each day. We dare not get distracted like the hare. At each step, we simply take what we can get and then move to the next step. According to an old Chinese proverb, "The person who removes a mountain begins by carrying away small stones."

Real change comes incrementally. If we wish to succeed we must understand this principle. Americans want everything yesterday; even Christians in our culture have not been immune to this malady. As I said before, we hate "compromise" with the world, and that is good. However, confusing incremental change with compromise is deadly to the advancement of any cause. Apart from the direct intervention of the Spirit of God, we will not see things change overnight in our culture.

Demanding all or nothing today is much like playing the lottery. It is not a wise strategy and it is highly unlikely to produce any of the results we desire. History consistently teaches this. Although we sometimes perceive dramatic, sweeping change, we must realize that we are seeing only the tip of the iceberg. Real change almost always occurs incrementally on the shoulders of individuals who have labored in relative obscurity and hardship over an extended period of time. The "dramatic, sweeping change" we occasionally see is merely the highly visible culmination of that process.

Real change almost always occurs incrementally.

For instance, the election of Ronald Reagan brought dramatic changes, not only to America, but to the world as well.[40] He seemed to burst onto the scene like an unstoppable juggernaut. And yet, the watershed event that led to Reagan's election in 1980 occurred in 1964 with the defeat of Barry Goldwater. If Goldwater had not run for President, it is highly unlikely that Ronald Reagan could have ever been elected sixteen years later. Goldwater energized conservatives. Many, like Don Hodel, who became Reagan's Secretary of Interior, got involved under Goldwater, stayed engaged in the process, and ultimately set the stage for Ronald Reagan's victory a decade and a half later, leading to what became known as the "Reagan Revolution."

Again, we often hear about how William Wilberforce, a member of the British Parliament, brought about the end of the slave trade in the British Empire in the early 1800s. It cost him twenty years of dogged persistence in the face of intense ridicule—even getting laughed off the floor of the Parliament by his peers. Victory, when it finally came, was dramatic, but it did not come cheaply or quickly.

Many baby steps over time lead to victory. If we are going to engage in the battle to restore God to His proper place in society, thereby restoring society itself, may we always choose to be tortoises, not hares. If we want to eat the entire elephant, we had better be prepared to do a lot of chewing for a long time to come. There is no substitute for perseverance. It is what births "dramatic change." It is what will birth a God-centered and moral society.

RULE #6: NO PAIN, NO GAIN.
CONTROVERSY IS MY FRIEND

I am often perplexed by the way Christians in the West think. Somehow we have gotten the nutty idea that God's blessing means we will be free from pain and persecution. Jesus didn't think that—He sweat drops of blood before being beaten and killed.[41] Peter didn't think that—he rejoiced that God had found him worthy to suffer for the name of Jesus.[42] Paul didn't think that—he was beaten, shipwrecked, imprisoned,

OPPOSITION IS ABSOLUTELY CRITICAL TO LONG-TERM SUCCESS.

tired, hungry, thirsty, cold and naked by his own account.[43]
They understood firsthand what pain was.

You cannot advance your cause
without pain.

In fact, they understood you cannot advance your cause
without pain. I believe our real problem in the West is we do
not love people deeply enough. We are willing to let others go
to hell for eternity in order to have them think well of us today.
But Jesus loved people too much to not be clear. They crucified
Him for it. Stephen loved people so deeply that he confronted
their sin. They stoned him for it. Peter was so passionate about
communicating God's love that he was beaten, imprisoned and
finally crucified upside down because he would not water down
the message.[44] Paul loved his fellow Jews so much that he said
he would willingly be damned for all time if it would save them
from an eternity apart from God.[45] They tried to kill him. What
each of these individuals had in common is they loved so deeply
they were willing to suffer for it.

But here is the bottom line: opposition is absolutely critical to long-term success. If we articulate a message contrary to
the status quo and experience no opposition, we can reasonably
conclude that our message was not heard. However, having said
that, a negative reaction from the opposition does not necessarily mean our message was heard and understood. It may be our
message was misunderstood, and the negative reaction was to a
message we did not at all intend.

For example, if we are overly strident in the presentation of our message, people may react to our style and never even hear our message. Or, we may talk about the necessity of being "born again," but what our secular audience hears is only that they must behave in a specified manner due to the cultural baggage they associate with the term. If I want to communicate with a Christian audience I can safely use the word "crusade," but if I want to talk with a Muslim prudence demands I find another term. We need to be wise in how we frame and present our message to secular and other non-Christian audiences.

> ## Controversy is my friend. I can use opposition to amplify my message.

However, if we properly present our message in terms that the culture can understand and still meet with resistance, we should be encouraged. In this case, opposition is a good indicator that our message is getting through. As Winston Churchill purportedly said, "You have enemies? Good. That means you've stood up for something, sometime in your life."[46]

I am reminded of an adage from the political arena: "The only bad press is no press at all." That statement may not be true in every circumstance, yet there is a lot of wisdom in it. A sure-fire way to lose is to allow our cause to be ignored. Even bad press is better than no press if it helps to raise the profile of our cause. However, it is then up to us to stay on message. In this sense, controversy is my friend. I can use opposition to amplify my message. If the opposition and media ignore us, our cause will die a premature death. Active opposition is critical to our long-term success because it catches people's attention. A reminder: if we control the rhetorical playing field forcing the opposition to react to our message they cannot win.

Consider Mel Gibson when he released *The Passion of the Christ*. He came under intense scrutiny. The movie caused a vehement reaction in some quarters. But Mel stayed on message. Ultimately, that reaction drove people into the theaters where they saw the movie. The controversy caused people to pay attention. Mel won.

Recently I was watching a news program. Dick Morris, a *former* advisor and *former* friend to Bill Clinton said that Hillary Clinton (a white woman) was playing the "race card" based on a statement she made earlier in the day. Later in the show, after he was gone, Geraldine Ferraro (a former Vice Presidential candidate) spent 15 minutes defending Hillary saying that what she said was not racist and that her statement was not a racist statement. She never got off defense. Dick must have been laughing to himself. She should have immediately accused Dick Morris of being a racist for trying to exploit race as a tool to divide the Democratic Party. The only thing she accomplished was continuing to raise the question in people's minds of the possibility that Hillary might be a racist. Those who want to believe the worst about Hillary will believe that she was a racist. Those who want to believe the best about Hillary will believe that she is not. For everyone else the controversy simply drove the question even deeper into their thinking. Geraldine lost. Dick won.

From time to time I have asked people whether or not they thought former U.S. Congressman Newt Gingrich was successful. I often get the response, "No! Nobody liked him." But then I ask, "What was his primary goal, and did he accomplish it?" Once the question is reframed in that manner, people begin to understand the difference between popularity and success. He created controversy through his "Contract with America," forcing the opposition to react. He then used the high-profile controversy as a platform to get his message out. Personal popularity had little to do with his strategies or actions. Popularity is nice and it can be helpful, but popularity is not the same as, nor necessarily essential to, success.

Consider Martin Luther King, Jr. Was he popular in the overarching culture? A majority of the dominant white culture considered him a nuisance and a troublemaker—particularly in the South. In fact, he was such an annoyance that someone felt it necessary to murder him in cold blood. While he was not very popular outside of the black community, he was immensely successful at moving his cause forward. He has become more popular since his death as the culture has recognized that he was right. The controversy took his life, but it also enabled him to move his cause forward.

Remember Jack Kevorkian, nicknamed "Dr. Death"? When he first came on the scene, the American public reacted negatively because he was promoting active euthanasia (intentional killing of patients often referred to as "mercy killing"). It did not take long until he was front and center on our television screens at night, and people began discussing the pros and cons of what he was advocating. Even if people did not agree with him, they became engaged in the debate that he had framed. As a result, Dr. Kevorkian steadily advanced his agenda with the general public even though he was a lightning rod for opposing moral views.

Finally, consider the apostle Paul. Was he well-liked, generally speaking, by the culture of his day? No! But was he successful? Few people in the history of the world have been more successful in accomplishing their goal. He and a handful of others turned the Roman world upside down. And yet, if ever there was a human lightning rod, it was Paul. He was stoned. He was beaten. He was flogged. But his opponents only served to amplify a well-framed message. Paul never confused popularity with success—and neither should we.

The irony is, bad press can be good if we are able to harness it to help move our cause forward.

Mel Gibson got bad press, as did Newt Gingrich, Martin Luther King, Jack Kevorkian, and the apostle Paul. The irony is, bad press can be good if we are able to harness it to help move our cause forward. If we have done our homework ahead of time, whether our press is good or bad, we should be able to advance our cause. Certainly I prefer good press, but I also understand the necessity of "bad" press as a tool for bringing about change. If I am willing to work hard to stay on message, to constantly reframe, controversy can be my greatest friend.

RULE #7: BE A LEADER, NOT A LONER
EVEN THE LONE RANGER HAD TONTO

In 1776, during the Continental Congress as the delegates were preparing to vote on the Declaration of Independence, Benjamin Franklin said, "We must hang together, gentlemen... else, we shall most assuredly hang separately."[47] If we are divided we cannot win. The opposition will pick us off and wear us down one by one. If we are united, win or lose, we will change the world in which we live. We dare not try to go it alone. We must either hang together or hang separately.

A few years ago I heard the story of a fraternity pledge class in San Diego. The fraternity members took all the pledges down to the beach and built a fire. Each pledge was given a cup of water to throw on the fire. One at a time each pledge emptied the contents of his cup onto the flames—with little effect. But then each pledge's cup was refilled. They were instructed to circle the bonfire, and when the word was given they were all to simultaneously empty their cups of water on the fire. This time the fire was snuffed out. Acting alone is almost always shortsighted. Acting together is critical to success.

There is an African proverb that goes something like this: "If you want to travel quickly, go alone. If you want to travel far, go together." We have a long way to go if we are going to make God the central overriding issue in our culture. It is not going to be quick or easy. We cannot go solo and dare hope for success. The task is too big for any one person to accomplish. The pressure is too great for one individual to carry alone.

If we are divided we cannot win.

Change can only occur as we work with others. Historically there have been two components to this: the cell group and the large group meeting. The large group meeting is where leaders communicate vision—where people can *feel* that they are part of something bigger than themselves. They get excited. They come away motivated. However, the cell group is where the majority of community, encouragement and ongoing training occurs. Historically, *the cell group is the most basic and indispensable building block of change*. Without it, a movement cannot be built, grown or succeed. Without an ongoing cell group structure a potential movement never amounts to anything more than a flash-in-the-pan. Thinking we can short-circuit that process and still be able to change culture is always a fatal mistake.

Even Jesus, as powerful and articulate as He was, could not do it alone since as a man he could only be in one place at one time. He was always building His life into people. The only times He was alone were when He was "alone" with His Father. His strategy was not to do all the work Himself—even though He was God. Rather His plan was to replicate His life, passion and relationship into the lives of others who would in turn re-cruit and train others. In this way the Kingdom of God could ultimately grow throughout the entire earth. Jesus was a leader, not a loner.

Jesus reinforced this in the lives of His disciples throughout His earthly ministry. He consistently sent them out in pairs to accomplish whatever task He assigned.[48]   Not only was Jesus not a loner, He did not want His disciples to be loners. About the only exception to this rule was when He sent Judas out to betray Him—alone.[49] If Jesus always sent out His disciples in pairs, we need to pay attention, both for our own good as well as the good of our cause. Be a leader, not a loner.

Change can only occur as we work with others.

I remember a situation where we helped one of the leading citizens of our city put on an evangelistic outreach event to which he invited the top 100 leaders in the city. Afterward, one of the attendees wrote him a letter expressing his extreme displeasure with a veiled threat to take legal action—a clear attempt to intimidate him into being quiet about Jesus. He did not respond personally. Instead, two other leading businessmen in the city set up an appointment with the disgruntled gentleman to graciously discuss the situation with him. Afterward, all threat of legal action vanished. Initially, the gentleman thought he could isolate, harass and bully one individual into silence. When he realized that attacking one person actually meant he would be attacking a *group of leaders clearly acting in unison*, he was no longer so aggressive.

However, merely working together is not enough. We must be of one heart and mind.   Ecclesiastes 4:12 says, "A person standing alone can be attacked and defeated, but two can stand back-to-back and conquer. Three are even better, for a triple-braided cord is not easily broken."[50] In a "braided" cord the strings are intertwined, not parallel. They give each other strength. They are inextricably connected. Jesus summed it up this way, "Just as I have loved you, you should love each other."[51] Jesus was a leader. Jesus was never a loner and he did not want His followers to be loners.

At the beginning of this chapter I referred to the British Parliamentarian, William Wilberforce, and the Clapham Sect. The Clapham Sect was a group of Christian business and intellectual leaders who used their resources and abilities to help Wilberforce succeed. (The name Clapham was adopted because that was the name of the section of London where these men happened to live.) Wilberforce was the mouthpiece. In the context of their love for Jesus Christ, they were all bound together by their passion to end the slave trade in the British Empire. Wilberforce was their leader but he was not a loner.

Change always comes with a price tag.

Change always comes with a price tag. Among those who knew the price and willingly paid it are Moses, Jesus, the apostle Paul, Vladimir Lenin, George Washington, William Wilberforce, Abraham Lincoln, and Martin Luther King. Like them, we do not know with certainty that we shall overcome (Jesus being the exception), but we do know without a doubt that if we do not make the attempt, we shall most certainly never succeed. History teaches, time and time again, that none who have advanced their cause have done so for free. A willingness to pay a price, stay on message, be persistent and work together, will greatly increase the likelihood of success

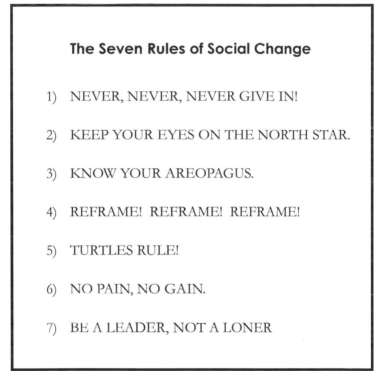

The Seven Rules of Social Change

1) NEVER, NEVER, NEVER GIVE IN!

2) KEEP YOUR EYES ON THE NORTH STAR.

3) KNOW YOUR AREOPAGUS.

4) REFRAME! REFRAME! REFRAME!

5) TURTLES RULE!

6) NO PAIN, NO GAIN.

7) BE A LEADER, NOT A LONER

Chapter 4 Review Questions

1. How willing would you be to become part of a "highly committed handful of individuals" whose goal was to make God the issue in a given area of our culture? What is the highest price you would be willing to pay to achieve this objective?

2. What is your reaction to learning that, with the exception of John, all the original disciples that Jesus commissioned (including Paul) were martyred for attempting to make God the issue in various cultures? Where in our world today do you see this spirit alive in the Christian church?

3. After reviewing the seven rules of social change presented in this chapter, which are the most important for you to adopt in your efforts to make an impact in your circle of influence? Why?

4. What is the difference between reframing and reacting in either personal or cultural debate?

5. How do opponents of Christianity help to further our message? What opportunities do they give us by opposing our message (if we will only take advantage of them)?

6. How can you actively work with others to advance the Kingdom of God more effectively than you are able to do on your own?

REFRAMING THE CULTURAL RHETORIC

"Be as shrewd as snakes and harmless as doves."
—Matthew 10:16

Words matter. Jesus knew this and therefore was always careful to speak wisely. If we wish to win the war for the culture, we must heed the words of Jesus to be "as shrewd as snakes and as innocent as doves" (Matthew 10:16).[52]

It is no secret that Christians consistently get "taken to the woodshed" by the secular media on cultural, ethical, social, and spiritual issues. In fact, the negative press is so bad that if I were a young adult today who grew up outside the church, I would probably believe that Christians oppose just about everything including tolerance, diversity, choice, separation of church and state—and maybe even happiness itself.

Now, many of you probably just responded by thinking, *"But we do oppose all of those things—except, of course, for happiness."* To which I say you are exactly right. And therein lies the problem. The broad culture perceives us as opposing just about everything, which prevents us from effectively communicating what we actually believe. (Keep in mind that perception constitutes reality for most people.) In fact, I think we often perceive ourselves as opposing just about everything, which shows that we are not the ones in control of the cultural rhetorical playing field. We are on defense, not offense. In effect, we have bought into the culture's perception of us! We spend the bulk of our efforts pulling up cultural "tares" rather than growing the wheat. It is now time for us to become "advocates" rather than "obstructionists" in the minds of our fellow countrymen. Instead of always objecting, we must shrewdly become perceived as "advocates" of diversity, tolerance, free speech, separation of church and state, and other areas where we are currently viewed as obstructionists. It is time for us to quit reacting, and start reframing. It is time for us to hijack every issue as a platform for our message.

We must become better at redefining the meaning of words than the modern-day revisionists themselves.

We must learn to aggressively reframe the rhetoric of the opposition, just as Jesus did. By this I mean that we unabashedly seize the opposition's rhetoric and give it additional or new meaning. We co-opt it. We redefine it. In fact, we must become better at redefining the meaning of words than the modern-day revisionists themselves. Redefining does two things. First, it broadens the meaning of the opposition's rhetoric to support and carry our message, while simultaneously diluting their original intent (I will flesh this concept out later in this chapter). Such is what happened to the term "family values" under Bill Clinton. (He redefined "family" to be something other than the traditional nuclear family.) It is also what the militant homosexuals have done to the term "diversity." They have broadened it beyond ethnicity and gender to include sexual behavior. They have literally hijacked the civil rights movement! Second, this approach moves the debate onto our playing field (making God the issue), thereby enabling us to control the rhetoric. This allows for forward progress instead of continually running into the proverbial "brick wall" because of a reactive mindset, which by its very nature is defensive.

If those around us fail to understand our message, then being right does our cause absolutely no good.

If we truly wish to win the cultural debate, being intellectually right is not enough. We have been right for a long time but we are still losing ground. How our fellow citizens perceive our words is just as important as being right. If those around us fail to understand our message, then being right does our cause absolutely no good.

One of the key components in the communication process is creating "linkage." Let me illustrate: A bumper sticker I routinely see says "Visualize World Peace"—not a bad slogan. But one day I saw another bumper sticker: "Visualize Whirled Peas." To this day, whenever I see the original bumper sticker I always recall its reworded, counterfeit cousin—and chuckle. That is linkage at work. I cannot think of one without thinking of the other.

Another example is the "Darwin" fish symbol, with evolutionary, leg-like appendages, which people stick on the back of their cars to mock the Christian "fish" symbol seen on other vehicles. It is difficult for me to see one symbol now without thinking of the other. This is another example of linkage.

Linkage is often a critical step in the reframing process. In the following pages I will illustrate how to create linkages by redefining cultural terminology, which should allow us to co-opt important issues of our day and reframe them to our advantage in the public debate.

Ultimately, creating linkage on various issues could enable us to achieve the perceived moral high ground (in addition to the *actual* moral high ground) within the culture. As you read, please keep in mind that I am not addressing legal or legislative strategies—only rhetorical posturing for making God the issue whether in large groups or one-on-one. The following examples are not intended to be exhaustive, but merely starting points for consideration.

The bottom line is that we must perceptually position ourselves as advocates rather than reactionaries—thereby enabling us to make the God of the Bible the issue.

Violence in Public Schools

For a long time now, many have used the increasing violence in public schools as a major vehicle for promoting stricter gun control. We can and should unapologetically turn this issue for our cause as well. I think it could become a powerful tool in our rhetorical arsenal, since all parents are concerned about the safety of their children.

Every time violence in public schools makes the front pages of the newspaper, we should unabashedly assert in our spheres of influence that in the public schools today, we Americans pretend that God is irrelevant to education, but then we act shocked when our children behave as if there really is no God.

The truth is, violence is a symptom of a person's beliefs (ultimately one's view of God), not a symptom of owning a gun. Our children are merely acting out what we have taught them by our silence as a culture about God. I believe this directly relates to why the great American educator, Noah Webster, known as "the Schoolmaster of the Nation," said, "Education is useless without the Bible."[53]

Both the pro-gun and anti-gun lobbies have missed the real point. Arming law-abiding citizens will not prevent another Columbine. Conversely, disarming the citizenry will not prevent it either as the high school massacre at Erfurt, Germany, on April 26, 2002, so horrifically demonstrated. Expelled student Robert Steinhaeuser gunned down thirteen teachers, two students, and a police officer at his former school.[54] This was the fourth time that a teen in Germany had killed school personnel or other students in a two-and-a-half-year period.[55] And this despite the fact that Germany imposes very strict gun control on its citizens.

It should, therefore, be relatively easy to make the rhetorical case that Columbine and Virginia Tech were caused by *censorship of religious speech, not guns,* since one's view of God will ultimately determine one's behavior. We hijack the gun control debate, creating linkage in order to inject our content and take control of the rhetoric.

We should be strategically prepared for any schoolhouse

> When the average parent in America
> comes to sincerely believe that the safety
> of his or her own children are at serious
> risk if God is not a part of education, then
> the opposition will be hard put to exclude
> "God" from the schools.

tragedy, of which there will undoubtedly be more since we live in a culture without a moral anchor. While emotions are still raw after such incidents and people are asking "Why?" we can make the connection for them. We must unequivocally place the blame for the tragedy where it belongs—at the feet of those who have removed the only sure foundation of morality from education. But we need to do this with great savvy and wisdom—and compassion.

When the average parent in America comes to sincerely believe that the safety of his or her own children are at serious risk if God is not a part of education, then the opposition will be hard put to exclude "God" from the schools. Fear for oneself is a powerful emotion, but not as powerful as a mother's fear for her children's safety.

Hate Crimes

When the opposition talks about hate crimes, we should talk about *hate crimes against people of faith* such as occurred at Columbine High School.[56] The "*people of faith*" addition broadens the rhetoric well beyond what the opposition will deem acceptable. We should link the phrase *"people of faith"* to the mantra of "hate crimes." Ultimately, the only way they will be able to combat us on this point (because of the linkage) will be to completely omit the phrase "hate crimes" or "hate speech" from their rhetoric— which they will not do, at least in the short term.

Although "hate crimes" legislation often includes hate crimes against *people of faith*, the latter is rarely the focus of the debate. Every official "hate crimes" panel or committee that is convened should be pressured to look at hate crimes against *people of faith* as well.

The opposition will often tend to react defensively (maybe even overreact), in a hypocritical attempt to keep God out of the debate. When they do, we may rightly ask why *people of faith* should not also enjoy the same Constitutional protections (civil rights) they are demanding for themselves. Why do they want to discriminate against God-fearing Americans? (Please remember, I am not trying to make the legal case; rather, I am reframing the perceptual case for the everyday public debate and conversation so that God becomes the central focus.)

Additionally, we should all drive home the point whenever we engage in dialogue on this issue that *"Hate crimes are symptoms."* They are no different from any other crimes in that they are merely symptomatic of a far more serious disease. That disease is the main message of this book: the fact that we have excluded God from the public square as the legitimate source of morality. Our culture—via government, education, and the media—has developed a God-phobia that seeks to ban every mention of God from public life. As a result, there is no rational basis for practicing respect instead of hate. Hate crimes are symptoms of teaching moral relativism, of teaching that people are not morally

Hate crimes are symptoms of failing to teach the only rationally defensible basis of moral obligation—God Himself.

accountable because there is no source of moral obligation in the universe. They are symptoms of teaching that human life has no inherent value because we are merely a by-product of "chance plus time," rather than the concern of a personal Creator. Hate crimes are symptoms of failing to teach the only rationally defensible basis of moral obligation—God Himself.

We should no longer let anyone talk about hate crimes, whether on television, in the workplace, or in our neighborhoods, without raising the issue of hate crimes and discrimination against *people of faith*, and then using it as a springboard to talk about the necessity of a wise God who is the only logical source of all moral obligation in the universe.

Tolerance

Similarly, when those who want to justify their immoral behavior talk about tolerance, we should reframe and broaden the focus of the dialogue to include *tolerance of all speech, including religious speech*. We should wrap ourselves in the mantle of being perceived as tolerant of all forms of legitimate speech, clearly implying that the opposition is "selective" and therefore promotes censorship (which they do). Anyone who claims to be tolerant but seeks to exclude speech with which they personally disagree is anything but tolerant. In the book *1984*, George Orwell referred to such two-faced talk as "doublespeak."

Within this context, the secularists will likely accuse us of intolerance and censorship when it comes to pornography. We should readily plead guilty to trying to protect the innocence of our children from being harmed—something our opposition does not seem to highly value. (If someone is foolish enough to publicly argue that free speech is more important than protecting our children, then give them all the rope they want to rhetorically hang themselves.) Then, without taking a breath, we can bring the question right back to their lack of tolerance and overt censorship of religious speech and whether we as Americans believe that such hateful intolerance is acceptable. (Remember, try to move back onto offense as quickly as possible.)

We must all daily redefine tolerance as being synonymous with free speech and then create linkage to religious speech by talking about "tolerance of religious speech." We should never miss the opportunity to link the two. This redefines "tolerance" with a new, broader meaning for the average uncritically thinking American—"free speech." Eventually, our neighbors and co-workers should never again hear the word "tolerance" without automatically equating it with "free speech" and "free religious speech." That is linkage. It also allows us once again to move to the "God" issue since we have now incorporated "religious" speech.

Diversity

We should all promote *ethnic and religious diversity* every chance we get. Like a savvy politician, we should take this issue away from the other side by pouring our meaning into it. By adding the terms "ethnic and religious" every single time the word "diversity" comes out of our mouth, we are again creating linkage. And we should make sure it comes out of our mouths every day so we can redefine it for the culture around us.

We do this for a number of reasons:

- First, it allows us to potentially co-opt the word "diversity," which our culture has already come to largely accept. The other side has worked hard to mainstream this term. Let's aggressively redefine it, giving it new meaning!

- Second, it allows us to isolate and expose what is primarily a sexually motivated agenda. This will force the opposition to make it obvious they really mean "sexual" diversity. So far we have let them piggyback sexual perversity on the back of legitimate diversity.

- Third, it allows us to get out in front on the issue of combating racism. This is not only culturally expedient, but it is the right thing to do in the eyes of God.

- Fourth, it allows us to inject religion (and therefore God) into the diversity debate. Much like the homosexuals have done, we overtly piggyback our meaning on the term.

At worst, our efforts will simply muddy the rhetorical waters. At best, we will successfully co-opt the term "diversity." Most importantly, it gives us control of the rhetorical playing field, adding another platform from which to talk about the

EDUCATION THAT
OMITS GOD IS
THE PRIMARY
INCUBATOR
FOR LYING,
CHEATING,
STEALING, AND
GREED.

"God of the Bible"—which is always the ultimate goal.

Terrorism

Many among the media elite are attempting to create linkage between theologically conservative Christians and the Islamic fundamentalists/terrorists. We should consistently counter with the charge that a person's view of God will determine how he treats others.

If we believe in a God who says, "Kill the infidel," we will likely hate those who do not believe as we do.

If we believe there is no God, like Adolph Hitler, then we are not obligated to treat anyone with kindness or tolerance because there is no rational source for moral obligation in the universe.

But if we believe in a God who says, "Love your enemies, do good to those who hate you,"[57] then we will be far more likely to extend kindness and respect wherever possible—and not just to those who happen to agree with us.

In this case, we are not creating linkage. Instead, we are hijacking the linkage that others are trying to create as a platform for our agenda—God.

Corporate Greed

Enron. Arthur Anderson. MCIWorldCom. For a while, the list seemed to grow daily. I have heard many people express their shock and dismay over the way many corporations blatantly lied to cover up mismanagement and outright greed on the part of executives. I fail to understand why people are shocked.

For the past thirty years, our universities have taught a form of ethics and morality that excludes God, who is the only rational source of moral obligation. Therefore, we should actually expect greedy self-serving behavior to be the norm, not the exception, whether it is visible to the public or not. If a person does not believe that God will hold him accountable for his actions, and if he believes it is not in his best self-interest to act in a moral manner why would he do so? After all, we live in an extremely self-focused "Just do it" culture.

More courses on business ethics might help, but not much. Greater oversight by the Securities and Exchange Commission is not the ultimate answer either. While onerous penalties might slow down certain expressions of greed and selfishness, they will never stop it. Those are merely Band-Aids applied to symptoms. Unless top corporate executives become convinced that God holds them morally accountable for their business decisions and actions in the marketplace, we will continue to breed more and more "Enrons" every day.

Education that omits "God" is the primary incubator for lying, cheating, stealing, and greed. The point is to link education that omits "God" with unethical and illegal corporate greed. Since people already feel strongly that corporate greed is evil (one of the few "evils" agreed upon by everyone in our culture), we create linkage between that and purely secular education.

President Theodore Roosevelt plainly understood this: "Progress has brought us both unbounded opportunities and unbridled difficulties. Thus, the measure of our civilization will not be that we have done much, but what we have done with that much. I believe that the next half century will determine if we will advance the cause of Christian civilization or revert to the horrors of brutal paganism. The thought of modern industry in the hands of Christian charity is a dream worth dreaming. The thought of industry in the hands of paganism is a nightmare beyond imagining. The choice between the two is upon us."[58]

Dishonesty in the Media

In an age when lies and deceit seem to be the norm, we should be quick to point out the connection between one's view of God and one's actions. Whether it is a President of the United States lying on the witness stand, or a reporter lying on the front page of the newspaper, we need to help our fellow citizens see the connection between God and truth. Widespread dishonesty is the result of our cultural view of God.

> Truth consistently takes a back seat to deadlines, personal agendas, ideologies and ambitions.

During my time in politics in our nation's capital, I would occasionally read an article in the newspaper covering a topic or event with which I was well acquainted. In about half of those articles, I observed factual errors—and that does not include the use of innuendo, intentional omission of crucial facts, or other rhetorical devises employed to distort the reader's perception. How much was the result of shoddy reporting and how much was intentional, I am not in a position to say. But what seems clear (especially in light of the book *Bias* by Bernard Goldberg, a former insider at CBS) is that truth consistently takes a back seat to deadlines, personal agendas, ideologies and ambitions.

Jayson Blair, a former reporter for the *New York Times*, is a blatant example. According to numerous reports, he routinely fabricated and plagiarized facts, stories, and sources for his articles. The *Times* was aware that he had a proclivity to lie and yet still kept him in their employ. Even William Safire of the *Times* confirmed on May 12, 2003, "We had plenty of warning." Clearly, truth is not the top priority at the *New York Times*. If it were, Mr. Blair would have been fired the first time he was caught lying in print. In my opinion, trusting a known liar to report the truth makes about as much sense as asking a convicted pedophile to take care of one's children.[59]

A fuzzy view of God will eventually lead to a fuzzy view of truth.

We should not be surprised by the secular media's willingness to deliberately distort truth or to be a complicit party in that process. Every poll I have seen over the last twenty years indicates that belief in God within the American press corps is substantially lower than among the general population. Therefore, we should actually expect truth to be a consistent casualty on the evening news and the front page of the newspaper. After all, a fuzzy view of God will eventually lead to a fuzzy view of truth. It is a simple matter of cause and effect. The two are directly linked and we should publicly point it out.

If we fail to connect the dots for our fellow citizens between personal integrity and one's view of God, then we will miss a great opportunity to point people back toward the God of the Bible who says, "Do not lie."

Abortion

A number of years ago I struck up a conversation with a young woman at an event I was attending. As we talked about God and abortion, I made sure I framed my message so that she could hear my heart and understand my intent. Near the end of our conversation she said, "You're one of those *compassionate* pro-lifers, aren't you?" Given her tone, she was clearly implying that in her view compassion was not a characteristic of most pro-lifers—how ironic. We must change this perception if we are to turn the battle on this issue, but it is not likely to happen through finger pointing (real or even perceived). Most importantly, we must use the issue to point women who have been personally touched by abortion toward the God of the Bible.

There are two potentially effective approaches we can use on this issue. The first is to aggressively make the case that most Americans believe the Bible is correct when it says that we are created in the image of God—that we all bear His image. Therefore, we should be very reluctant to destroy that image without just cause.[60] Aborting the image of God should be rare because we choose to make it rare. The linkage is between the words "abortion" and the "image of God" within the context of "choice." Juxtaposing the two images allows us to reframe the issue. Our justification once again is based on God Himself.

The point is to drive home the "image of God" rhetoric into the psyche of each and every American. We want to quickly move as many Americans as possible toward overtly viewing the

Bible and the God of the Bible as the most legitimate source of moral authority. (Ultimately, we want them to view the God of the Bible as the sole source of legitimate moral authority.) We can use this issue to help in that process.

We can then casually tag on the thought that although abortion may be a "necessary evil" in some cases, it does not have to be a "widespread evil" in American society. This last turn of phrase allows us to sound reasonable while planting or reinforcing the thought in the listener's mind that abortion really is an "evil." At the proper time when the culture is ready, we can drop the word "necessary." As we engage the culture on this and many other issues keep in mind that we are trying to eat an elephant—a really big elephant.

For rhetorical purposes, we should generally avoid talking about "legislating" morality; rather, we are simply "promoting" morality and trying to preserve the "image of God." Most Americans would agree that we should "promote" morality. And if we say this nicely, in a non-confrontational way—a compassionate way—the American people should be able to hear our words.

This rhetoric accomplishes two things. First, it allows us to show once again how "God" relates to real-life decisions in a way that the average American can hear. We all like to hear that we have intrinsic worth in God's eyes. That is a very positive message that we should all attempt to emphasize whenever possible. In addition, 85 percent of Americans say they believe in the "God of the Bible," so we simply link the two beliefs by stating the Bible says that we are created in the image of God. This may well give us the ability to move people's thinking on the issue itself because of the likely conclusion they themselves will reach over time. But most importantly, it allows us to once again posit "God" as the focal point.

However, there may be a far more emotionally powerful argument that can be made. The plague of abortion has sown the seeds of its own demise. There are a great many women who are suffering emotionally (including recurring nightmares) because of abortions they had when they were younger. Strategically highlighting their personal experiences in the context of the forgiveness only God can provide can have two very tangible effects.

We now live in a culture where emotional arguments hold more weight than intellectual ones.

First, it would allow us to reach out to those women who are hurting emotionally as the result of an abortion, offering them God's love, forgiveness, and healing.

Second, if properly framed, it could move us as a culture well down the path to making abortions "rare" through young women exercising their "choice" not to have an abortion. We now live in a culture where emotional arguments hold more weight than intellectual ones. Pain is a powerful emotional argument. When confronted with the reality of the potential emotional pain that abortion can bring, many young women may well decide, of their own accord, to avoid such pain.

But most importantly, in this process, many wounded women (both those who have had abortions and those who are considering one) may finally find the love and forgiveness for which they are so desperately searching. Extending love (and being perceived as extending love) rather than condemnation is the model God has given us in Jesus Christ. In essence we link their pain (or potential pain) to abortion, while linking emotional healing to God.

The people who need to lead in the process are the women who have been personally wounded by this harmful plague but have since experienced God's overwhelming love, forgiveness, and healing. The rest of us need to do everything we can to actively support them—through prayer, unconditional acceptance, finances, administrative support, and continual words of encouragement.

Homosexual Behavior

This is the toughest issue we are going to face over the next decade. The other side is well organized and has refined their message and the machinery to deliver it.

A while ago I sat down behind closed doors with a leading national political figure who is a follower of Jesus Christ. With pain on his face, he said that the last time he spoke up criticizing homosexual behavior, he got hammered in the news media every single day for the following six months. I have not heard him say anything about homosexual behavior recently. And he is not unique in his experience among Christians operating in the political arena.

Not long ago I had lunch with a prominent banker. We began talking about some of the challenges he faces as a Christian in the marketplace. In that context the issue arose of "benefits for domestic partners" (wherein the partners of practicing homosexual employees receive the same corporate benefits as do the married spouses of heterosexual employees). He was straightforward. He said that so far his company had been able to resist, but that it was coming at them "like a freight train."

If we accept the current terms of engagement regarding homosexual behavior in our culture today, we will lose, just like we lost the battle over abortion. Given our current rhetorical posture, we are going to get run over by it—unless we can co-opt it.

Rhetorically, we must stop viewing homosexual behavior primarily as an issue to be confronted and addressed. Pagans are going to act like pagans no matter what we do. Instead, we must begin to view homosexual behavior as a platform from which to discuss God. This will require varied strategies depending upon the setting, but the goal in each case will be to co-opt the issue, not to react to it. In many cases, we must strategically ignore the issue itself. Following are some examples:

- When homosexuals hold a Day of Silence in your school, avoid reacting. Instead think of how you can shrewdly hijack it. For instance, make up T-shirts that say *"Silent no more. Stop the genocide in Darfur!"* Of course, the genocide in Darfur is against Christians. This allows you to stand in solidarity with our brothers and sisters in Christ who are being persecuted while simultaneously co-opting the intent of the Day of Silence for the cause of those suffering for the name of Christ. Opposing genocide is always a popular cause, which makes it

> If we accept the current terms of engagement regarding homosexual behavior in our culture today, we will lose, just like we lost the battle over abortion.

difficult to criticize without looking reactionary. Make sure the T-shirts are all the same color and immediately recognizable. If you can get a 20-30 of your friends in your school to wear them you can hijack the Day of Silence for the cause of Christ without ever saying a negative word about homosexual behavior. The point is, figure out a way to hijack the platform, moving from defense to offense. Force them to debate your issue. Never debate theirs. Don't react. Remember, controversy is your friend if you stay on message—especially if reporters show up.

• When homosexuals hold sensitivity training classes in Corporation XYZ, we graciously demand equal opportunity to talk about how to be sensitive to the feelings of *people of faith*—especially with employers who are sympathetic to our cause. If Corporation XYZ does not cooperate we publicly chastise them (with a reasonable tone in our voice and a warm smile on our face) for actively promoting intolerance against *people of faith*.

• When the United Way tries to eliminate funding for the Boy Scouts because they do not allow people who engage in homosexual behavior to be scout leaders, we publicly accuse the United Way of censorship, bigotry, and of being "intolerant" of religious belief (all of which would be true). Then we strongly request that, in order to show that they really are tolerant and sorry for such hateful, anti-religious bigotry, they give money to a designated Christian charity that feeds the poor. At least give them enough of a black eye that many *people of faith* will be more likely to give their donations to another group next year—not the United Way.

• When homosexuals in a high school show up in the office of their state legislator demanding his or her assistance, he or she should turn the tables by asking if they will first co-sponsor a debate on the basis of morality in their school, since that seems to be the underlying point of contention. Any reluctance on their part should be framed as hypocritical bigotry and intolerance. Never say you won't assist them. Instead, demand they embrace your agenda because it is the underlying question—the issue that must be settled first. Even Christian students on a high school campus could use this strategy to sponsor a public debate in front of the entire student body.[61]

- When secularists introduce hate crime and hate speech legislation, we should attempt to attach amendments to those bills stating that the bill "should in nowise be construed to restrict religious speech." When they oppose us we can publicly ask why they want to censor the speech of *people of faith*. To be successful, we must always keep the other side on the defensive.

The one thing we must never, never, never do, is allow the debate to become focused on homosexual behavior. It puts us on the defense. Debating homosexual behavior apart from the larger context of God is nothing more than a spitting match. If we want to turn the cultural tide, we must rapidly transition to offense. We cannot stop a freight train barreling down on us, but we can strategically derail or hijack it to make God the issue.

Debating homosexual behavior apart from the larger context of God is nothing more than a spitting match.

Morality

Finally, when secularists talk about morality in any context, we can respond by saying, *"Morality is merely a fairy tale on the level of the tooth fairy unless God exists.* Teaching values apart from God is like explaining how a light bulb works without ever mentioning electricity, or talking about how the automobile runs but never referring to the internal combustion engine. Talking about values and morality is meaningless if divorced from their source. If there is no God, we are simply arguing about conflicting preferences, not right and wrong, not good and evil. Right and wrong cease to exist the moment God is removed from the equation.

To drive the point home, we can quote Adolph Hitler, who said, "Success is the sole earthly judge of right and wrong."[62] If the God of the Bible does not exist, then what rational basis do we have for condemning Hitler's words and actions? I may "feel" that he was wrong, but that does not make him wrong. All it means is that I feel a certain way. It is a morally non-compelling statement without teeth. And if Hitler were alive today, I certainly doubt he would care about how I "feel."

Right and wrong cease to exist the moment God is removed from the equation.

This gives us the opportunity to point out that if God does not exist, then Adolph Hitler did not do anything morally wrong. Again, we create linkage between one's behavior and one's source of moral belief. We need to be able to rhetorically demonstrate that even attempting to teach morality (including "tolerance") without first positing "God" is futile and ridiculous, because morality apart from God is no more than a child's fairy tale. If God does not exist, I am not obligated to act in a moral fashion. Not only are those words true, they are absolutely horrifying when viewed through the eyes of history. This is a message that we must imbed in our rhetoric whenever we discuss moral issues. We must show that behavior follows belief.

If God does not exist, then Adolph Hitler did not do anything morally wrong.

At some point someone will likely claim it is a false argument to say that if the God of the Bible does not exist, then we have no basis for condemning Hitler, since there are many other religions in the world from which morality can be learned. The simplest response is to reply, "I don't believe in polytheism, pantheism, or a God who says, "Kill the infidel." Therefore, if you can prove to me beyond a reasonable doubt that the God of the Bible does not exist, I will change my position on homosexual behavior, pedophilia, abortion, incest, pornography, rape, murder, lying, cheating, stealing, and even genocide.["][iii] The point is to use the issue to keep the focus on the God of the Bible, not to give other religious beliefs a platform.

Separation of Church and State

We will inevitably be accused of trying to violate the so-called doctrine of "separation of church and state" as we advance the "God" issue. When we are so accused, we should forthrightly seize the phrase as our own in order to redefine it. (Let me remind the reader that I say this from a rhetorical perspective, not a legal one.) We do ourselves no favors by rowing upstream trying to argue against separation of church and state. Whether we like it or not, the average American believes in it.

[iii] In order to prove that the God of the Bible does not exist, they must first disprove the resurrection of Jesus Christ based on the historical evidence—a truly difficult task for someone who is intellectually honest.

Therefore, they should perceive us as "believing" in it as well. After all, people do not resist their own ideas. We should boldly steal the rhetoric from the opposition and then redefine it just like the anti-God revisionists do to us all the time. We can do this without compromising our beliefs at all.

We can shrewdly respond by saying that we, along with Thomas Jefferson, *strongly* believe in separation of church and state. Jefferson believed that the federal government should have no jurisdiction over religion or religious speech. In 1798, he wrote, "No power over the freedom of religion...[is] delegated to the United States by the Constitution."[63]

Thomas Jefferson advocated separation of church and state. However, groups like the American Civil Liberties Union (ACLU) seem to agitate for "*segregation* of church and state." Jefferson believed in freedom *of* religion whereas the ACLU lobbies for freedom *from* religion. Thomas Jefferson's primary concern was to *protect and promote* religious speech, whereas the ACLU pushes the federal government and the courts to *censor* religious speech—especially in education.

Jefferson believed liberty must have a rational basis. The ACLU apparently would argue, "Liberty happens." Portions of the following statement, made by Thomas Jefferson in 1781, are engraved on the Jefferson Memorial in Washington, D.C.: "God who gave us life gave us liberty. And can the liberties of a nation be thought secure when we have removed their only firm basis, a conviction in the minds of the people that these liberties are the Gift of God?"[64]

Thomas Jefferson believed morality needed a solid foundation. The ACLU apparently believes, along with Adolph Hitler, that something other than God "is the sole earthly judge of right and wrong." (I would be fascinated to know what, or who, they think is that ultimate arbiter of good and evil.) In this regard, I strongly suspect that Jefferson himself would agree that *segregation* of church and state was the primary cause of the Columbine and Virginia Tech massacres, as well as most of the violent behavior in public schools today.

The anti-God opposition has heavily promoted Thomas Jefferson, making him their poster child. It's time we recapture him and make him ours—thereby outflanking the opposition. It's a lot less work than rowing upstream.

The goal is to begin giving the phrase "separation of church and state" a new *perceived* meaning for the average citizen. We do this by first recasting the opposition's use of the term as "*segregation* of church and state," and then accusing them of censorship of religious speech—which is what they do. Again, the worst-case scenario is that raising the issue of "*segregation* of church and state" will simply muddy the waters. Given the current perceptual climate, that would be an improvement. However, the best-case scenario is that it will be a one-two punch that will inflict great damage on the opposition. Most importantly, however, it will give us control of the rhetorical playing field in order to more effectively make God the issue.

"*Segregation* of church and state" is a phrase we need to drive home every chance we get if we wish to reopen arenas that are currently closed or are closing to "God" speech. And it is easy to do. When a teacher brings up separation of church and state, a student can simply reframe it. When a school board member or principal espouses separation of church and state, a parent can easily turn the issue with this phrase. The potential applications are numerous. This brings to mind the words of the late Rev. E. V. Hill, who pastored Mt. Zion Missionary Baptist Church in Los Angeles: "If you want to make a point, use a sledgehammer." This is one phrase where we should unabashedly employ the E.V. Hill sledgehammer method of communication as often as possible.

If we can successfully undercut the anti-God opposition by boldly seizing this one phrase, I believe we can leapfrog forward in the war to inject the God of the Bible back into the culture, including public education, thereby reestablishing a rational basis for morality.

There may well be a receptive audience for the use of this phrase. As Democratic U.S. Senator Joseph Lieberman said, "The line between church and state is an important one, and has always been critical for us to draw. But in recent years I fear we've gone far beyond what the framers imagined in separating the two."[65] We need to create a rhetorical environment where we turn the existing perception on its head.

Conclusion

All the preceding examples have one purpose: to demonstrate how we can confront American culture with the God of the Bible. Through creating linkage wherever possible, or at least using cultural issues as springboards, we give ourselves a platform from which to talk about God in a manner that the culture can understand and potentially embrace.

Our responses should always intentionally move us away from an argument we cannot *perceptually* win within the current cultural context, to a place where we can redefine the perceptual terms of the entire debate. In every scenario, our goal is always to make the God of the Bible the issue. Once God becomes the watershed issue, we can then, and only then, begin to pour substantive content into the debate. Remember the watchword of this strategy: Reframe!

Chapter 5 Review Questions

1. Why does being "right" not ensure success? If we are right about God, yet are not changing our culture, what are we lacking?

2. How would you define the effectiveness of "linkages" in reframing the cultural debate? Which of the examples given in this chapter could you most easily appropriate?

3. Cite an instance when you responded

defensively to an opponent of God. How might you have reframed the issue to put your opponent on the defensive and make God the issue? What linkage could you have employed?

4. Why is God the central issue in all discussions regarding cultural ills such as intolerance, hate crimes, racism, and others? How can any discussion about these issues be reframed to make God the focus?

5. How does the manner in which we present God (compassionately vs. arrogantly) make a difference in how our opponents respond to what we say?

CHAPTER 6

MAKING GOD THE ISSUE

"We can trace all of our human problems
to our view of God."
—Bill Bright

Benjamin Franklin said, "The definition of insanity is doing the same thing over and over and expecting different results."[66]   For too long we have been tilting with windmills believing that if we just try harder we can somehow win back the culture. I'm not saying we should quit defending life created in God's image, or give up defending the God ordained institution of marriage, or abandon the battle for racial reconciliation (Jesus commanded us to love one another).

I am saying the battles for our moral sanity are ultimately doomed to failure if we do not engage the culture in a simultaneous conversation about who God really is and why it matters. It is time to unapologetically hijack every cultural symptom as a platform for making God the issue in the public square just as Jesus, Peter and Paul did. No matter the question, is it time to reframe the pivotal issue as "God."

For example, which of the following statements do you think are more effective in modern culture:

- Abortion is wrong.

- Abortion is okay—unless the God of the Bible actually exists.

- Homosexual behavior is wrong.

- Homosexual behavior is okay—unless the God of the Bible actually exists.

- Racism is wrong.

- Racism is okay—unless the God of the Bible actually exists.

- Pedophilia is wrong.

- Pedophilia is okay—unless the God of the Bible actually exists.

- Stealing is wrong.

- Stealing is okay—unless the God of the Bible actually exists.

I think you get the point. It is time to aggressively recon-

> The battles for our moral sanity are
> ultimately doomed to failure if we do not
> engage the culture in a simultaneous
> conversation about who God really is and
> why it matters.

nect America's moral compass to the underlying conversation of who God is. We need to intentionally hijack the conversation. It's a huge task. Getting started can feel daunting. It will certainly take us out of our comfort zone. It may even be a bit scary. But in order to accomplish anything in life you always have to take that first step. But remember, we don't have to eat the entire elephant in one bite. All we have to do today is take the next step.

In Chapter 4 under the seventh rule of social change I said, *"The cell group is the most basic and indispensible building block of a movement."* It is the most effective vehicle for involving others in a movement and therefore is the most effective tool for bringing about change. It is not just a *Kum-ba-yah group* where everyone sits around the campfire holding hands. Rather, it is an *Action group* where everyone's hands are strengthened in pursuit of a cause. Never underestimate the long-term power of a cell group that is focused on a goal. The cell group is the incubator for change. Without it, change falters and shrivels. The cell group is where ideas put down deep roots. It is where abstract concepts transform into concrete action. It is where the cause is embraced and owned. It is where lifelong relationships are forged. It is where lasting commitment is bred. It is the life-blood of a movement.

Do you want to help change the course of history in America? Start a cell group with the intention of training people (including yourself) to make God the issue in their sphere of influence. How you get started doesn't really matter. Where you end up makes all the difference. Ask a few friends to come over for pizza on Friday night, and then engage them in conversation about who they think God is. Give your friends an opportunity to be a part of the solution by joining with you in learning more about how to make God the issue in their spheres of influence. The point is, to get started you have to ask others to come along with you. You may only be able to find one other person. Great! Get started. Don't put it off.

So you ask, "Once I have my group, what do I do?" Great question.

My dad once made the statement, *"We can trace all our human problems to our view of God."* If it is true that all of our problems really come from an inaccurate view of God, where do you think is the logical place to start? I would answer, "With my view of God." Only after I have begun growing in my intellectual and personal understanding of *who God really is and why it matters* would I shift my focus to engaging with the culture. However, you will need to size up the situation for your group. For instance, if what you are excited about is going after the culture—start there. Allow your natural motivation to drive you through the process. You are much more likely to make it through to the end. I will unfold the process in the following pages in its logical progression so you can see how the process builds on itself. But again, start at the point where you are personally most highly motivated—you can always go back and fill in the gaps.

In the Body of Christ today in the West, most of us do not really know who God is, and therefore, we do not really know how to effectively explain to someone else who God is. Too often we pursue a false god who makes us feel good about ourselves rather than a loving God who challenges us to grow beyond our self-centeredness. We choose to follow a seductive god who says, "Learn to love yourself so that you can love others and God," rather than a wise God who says, "Learn to love God and others, which is the only way you will ever really learn to love yourself." Other times, we opt for a compassionless God of exacting justice who more closely resembles the god who says, "Kill the infidel!" than the God who says, "Love your enemies. Do good to those who hate you." No wonder we consistently fail to effectively communicate to our culture who God really is.

Unlike the federal government, you cannot give away what you do not own.

As followers of Jesus, we will never be able to effectively make the God of the Bible the issue in our culture if we do not personally pursue a deeper understanding of who He is. Let me restate that a slight bit differently. As followers of Jesus, we will **_NEVER_** be able to effectively make the God of the Bible the issue in our culture if we do not personally pursue a deeper understanding of who He is. What I mean by NEVER is: not ever; not under any condition; no way. Unlike the federal government, you cannot give away what you do not own.

WE MUST KNOW WHO GOD REALLY IS

First, we must have an actual working knowledge of who God really is. Don't assume you already have this one down pat—you are likely to be very surprised (I'll tell you my own story in this regard later on). Put your roots down deep into God's character and then learn to intentionally apply that understanding to your daily life. This is critical, because our view of God is the foundation of how we live our lives. It determines everything else. And again, you cannot give away what you do not own.

> The only way to truly change who we are is to change our view of God.

Too many of us have a view of God heavily shaped by our culture and how we feel rather than by who God, Himself, says He is. This is what has led to so many of our personal and societal dysfunctions. Our solution is often to try to fix our dysfunctions, or even worse, we rationalize our behavior in order to help us cope with life, when in reality the only way to truly change who we are is to change our view of God. It is a clear *cause & effect* relationship.

I have observed an amazing dynamic over and over again: as a person's view of God changes, that person is changed (this is also true for culture). However, we often try to cure the disease by suppressing the symptoms. How much sense does that make? It's like trying to keep a pot from boiling over by clamping down the lid tighter and tighter rather than by reducing the source of the heat. Unless you reduce the heat, sooner or later the lid will blow. Again, it is a simple issue of *cause & effect*. But here is the real bottom line: you cannot give away what you do not have. If you do not understand who God really is, you will **NEVER** be able to point others to who God actually is. In fact, you will probably end up inadvertently misleading them.

So you may honestly respond, *"I think I have a pretty solid view of who God is."* If that is you, indulge me for a moment and let me relate to you a couple stories from my own life and then follow up each story with some questions. Are you game? Here goes.

A little over ten years ago, I was struggling to make some major decisions about the next step in my life. A friend of mine suggested that we head up to Canada just to get away for a couple days to talk. At that point my felt need for wise advice was at an all-time high so I jumped at the opportunity. By the end of the first day, after walking the streets of Victoria, B.C, my friend turned to me and said, "Brad, your intellectual theology is great." Although I was not so brash as to verbalize it, I was in total agreement with him. Inside I was nodding my head, "Yes, it is." But then the other shoe dropped. I should have seen it coming, but sometimes we only see what we want to see. He said, "But *your* application stinks." I turned to him, and since he was a friend, I said humorously but also seriously, "Those are fighting words. You need to either put up or shut up." Thirty minutes later I cried "Uncle."

So, let me ask you, how is your application? Do you really *love* sinners as Jesus did or do you deep down inside resent them? Jesus said, "Follow me and I will make you fishers of men." Are you fishing? And when you fish, do you fish out of compassion (as Jesus did) or obligation? (Yeah, I admit it, I feel a little convicted too. Of course, that means that even now, I still have a lot of work to do on how I view ~~others~~ God.)

Next story. About twenty-five years ago, I was with my dad in his office while he was being interviewed by a reporter from a Christian magazine. At one point the reporter asked my dad, "Dr. Bright, tell us a problem you face that the average 'Joe Christian' can relate to." My dad promptly responded, "I don't have any problems." To which the reporter countered, "Dr. Bright, don't over-spiritualize. Everyone has problems."

Well...the reporter ended up asking the question seven times, each time trying to phrase it a little differently to see if he could get through what he perceived as my dad's overly pious facade. However, my dad finally turned to the young man and said words I will never forget: "You need to understand something. I am a slave—a slave of Jesus. A slave has no rights. The only obligation of the slave is to do whatever his master asks him to do. It is not the slave's responsibility to be successful, only obedient. Once you understand this, you understand you do not have any problems, you only have opportunities to see God work."[67]

That was one of those "Aha moments" in my life. In an instant I understood my father in a way I never had before. I immediately sensed he was not talking from his head; rather he was speaking straight from his heart. Suddenly, I got it! Now it

THE NEXT
TIME YOU FACE
SOMETHING YOU
TRULY BELIEVE
IS A PROBLEM
ASK YOURSELF
THE FOLLOWING
QUESTION,
"WHAT ATTRIBUTE
OF GOD DO I
NOT REALLY
BELIEVE IS
TRUE IN THIS
SITUATION?"

made sense how he could go through incredibly stressful situations and never lose a moment's sleep. It was a heart-felt statement based on following closely on the heels of his Master over a period of three decades. It was in that moment I came to understand the true "genius" of Bill Bright. He honestly believed on the gut level that he had no problems because every challenging situation was merely another "opportunity" to see his Master work.

It is our view of God that inevitably shapes who we are.

So I ask you, do you have problems or opportunities to see God work? Be honest. Only you and God are listening. Now, here's the kicker. If you have "problems," your view of God is flawed. Ouch! Either you don't believe He is totally sovereign or that He really is all-powerful or that He is perfectly loving. Somewhere your intellectual or heart view of God is off base. The next time you face something you truly believe is a "problem" ask yourself the following question, *"What attribute of God do I not really believe is true in this situation?"* (By the way, this is a great question to ask as well when you're worried, feeling hopeless, or angry at someone.) Never forget, life is not about you, rather it is all about who God is. It is our view of God that inevitably shapes who we are. Until you truly learn that lesson you are destined to always have "problems."

So, how is your view of God? Does it need a little work? Yeah, so does mine. For me, I'm sure it will take more than a lifetime to get my view of God to match with the reality of who He really is—but I am making progress. You can too.

I could tell you many other stories that would probably be helpful for you and humbling for me, but my only goal at this juncture is to get you pointed in the right direction. So, may I make a recommendation? Go to www.DiscoverGod.com. Sign up for the daily eDevotional that focuses on the character of God. Download (for free) one of the small group studies on the attributes of God. Click on one of the video clips of Bill Bright talking about who God is and why it matters—listen to one each week. Or go to the Resources section where we list materials by others who have written on this subject as well. But remember, don't try to eat the whole elephant today. Just take another bite. Remember the story of the tortoise and the hare? Turtles rule!

WE MUST BE EMPOWERED BY GOD'S SPIRIT

The second step to effectively making God the issue is to allow God's Spirit to empower you. Again, don't assume you know this one either. Just because you know who the Holy Spirit is, or because you have had some kind of emotional experience does not mean you understand how to be empowered by the Spirit of God for service every moment of every day. This is critical because you are not capable of living the Christian life. And again, you cannot give away what you do not own.

Imagine for a moment that you're a surfer, plummeting down a massive wave. It is the ultimate rush! Simply by remaining on the face of the wave, the incredible power of the ocean thrusts you forward at incredible speeds. Sound simple? The concept is. But have you ever thought about what it takes to stay on the wave? Focus. Practice. Risk. Perseverance. Time. Effort. Courage. But the end result is sheer exhilaration as the surfer rides the power of the mighty ocean itself.

This is exactly what John 15:5 is all about. Jesus said, "I am the vine, you are the branches. Those who remain in me, and I in them will produce much fruit. For apart from me you can do nothing." Remaining in the vine, like riding a wave, is not a passive process. It is active. It requires effort. It takes practice. It involves risk. It requires being intentional. It is a deliberate choice. But in the end we experience the sheer exhilaration of God's power carrying us forward by His Spirit.

Too often we try to "live the Christian life" in our own strength, attempting to push the ocean, paddling along with all our might. But we miss out on the total thrill of riding the wave of God's Spirit allowing His power to thrust us forward. Both require effort. But the first focuses on *living (or doing)* the Christian life. This always leads to frustration. For the sake of clarity, let me repeat that with emphasis. This **ALWAYS** leads to frustration. The second focuses on developing our relationship with Jesus while trusting God to empower us by the limitless power of His Spirit. It is the key to living supernaturally—to riding the wave.

So, are you riding the wave or pushing the ocean? The answer is not to paddle harder. You will never be able to paddle hard enough to please God. Rather the answer is to discover God, Himself. Discover who God *really* is and learn how to allow His Spirit to empower you. Then (and only then) will you be set free to discover the full and unleashed power of His Spirit. As followers of Jesus, our only job is to ride the wave of His Spirit—and it is the one thing we should do with all our might! Quit paddling and start riding.

The story is told of a warrior of towering reputation. His enemies feared him greatly. More than anything else, they feared his sword, whose power had inspired wild rumors and legends. After hearing enough of these wild tales, his king finally demanded an examination of the notorious battle weapon. The warrior had his celebrated sword delivered to the palace by special messenger. The king examined the weapon closely before finally sending back this message: "I see nothing wonderful in the sword; I cannot understand why any man should be afraid of it." The warrior must have smiled as he read the king's words, for he replied, "Your Majesty has been pleased to examine the sword, but I did not send the arm that wielded it. If you had examined that, you would have understood the mystery."[68]

You and I have each been given a sword. But our sword will only be as effective as the person wielding it. Will you wield your own sword, or will you let the Spirit of God wield it through you?

About fifteen years ago I decided to read one of my dad's books on the Spirit-filled life entitled The Secret (not to be confused with the more recent book by the same name). I figured I knew everything that was in it since I had heard my dad talk about the Spirit-filled life since I was a child. However, I didn't

> ### The Bible is very clear that the primary role of the Holy Spirit in our lives is to empower us for service.

want to hurt my dad's feelings, so I read it (God is often very creative in how He motivates us).

A few weeks later I picked up a book by Dwight L. Moody (regarded by many as the greatest evangelist of the 19th century) entitled *Secret Power*, written 120 years prior to my dad's book. I was struck by his same focus on the absolute necessity of being empowered by the Spirit of God in order to even be able to live the Christian life. And then it dawned on me in a new way: God's truth never changes because God Himself never changes.

The Spirit-filled life is what enabled the believers of the first century to change their world. It is what empowered Dwight L. Moody to preach with power. It was this "secret" Bill Bright discovered that made him a powerful tool in the hands of his Master.

The Bible is very clear that the primary role of the Holy Spirit in our lives is to empower us for service. If you want God to use you to help change the world, don't live the Christian life another day in your own strength. You're not strong enough. No one is.

If no one has ever explained to you how to be filled and empowered with the Holy Spirit on a moment by moment basis, go to the Discover God website (www.discovergod.com) and click on the section "Discover God's Power" where you can find resources that will help you in understanding how to allow God's Spirit to live through you. An accurate understanding of who God is combined with an understanding of the Spirit-filled life will set you free to change your world.

WE MUST KNOW HOW TO INTRODUCE OTHERS TO GOD

The third step in making God the issue is to make sure you know how to effectively explain to someone else how they can begin a relationship with God though Jesus. This should become so second nature that you can do it in your sleep.

Most of us do not know how to clearly explain to someone else how they can begin a relationship with the awesome creator God of the universe. In fact, most of us don't even know how to tell someone else our own story of how we began our relationship with God. If I do not know how to introduce someone else to God, I can **NEVER** really close the loop in making Him the issue in someone else's life.

There are many ways to explain to another person how to begin a relationship with God. I like to use the *Four Spiritual Laws* (Disclaimer: my dad wrote it so I admit my bias). Other people prefer to use *Evangelism Explosion*. Still others prefer Billy Graham's booklet *"Five Steps to Peace with God."* Whatever method you use, keep it simple and concise. Also, make sure you can tell your own story of how you began your relationship with God in a concise and interesting way (practice on a friend). Finally, leave something with them to read or review on their own after you have left. But, to the best of your ability, be friendly and clear, then leave the results to God.

If you can, find someone in your church or community who introduces people to Jesus on a regular basis and ask them to coach you. Make sure you find someone who is actually doing it themselves and seeing results, not just talking about doing it. This is crucial. Remember, a person cannot give away what they do not own. If they are not doing it or they are not effective, they cannot teach you because they do not know themselves. You can quickly ascertain this by simply asking them to tell you a couple stories about situations they have been in over the last few months where they have been able to *personally* introduce someone to Jesus. If they can't tell you any such stories, don't make a big issue of it. Don't embarrass them. Just move on. Find someone who can. If you really cannot find anyone, email us at discovergod@ccci.org and we will try to connect you with someone in your area who can coach you.

WE MUST KNOW HOW TO MAKE GOD THE ISSUE

The fourth step in making God the issue is to actually learn how to make God the issue in any situation. That is what this book has been all about. Learn to reframe effectively so that you can take advantage of any opportunity, anywhere, any time. Come up with various scenarios and practice with your friends. Learn to look at everything as a platform for talking with others about their view of God. Learn to think differently. Quit reacting to the culture.

The key to change is learning
to think differently.

For this purpose, let me recommend that you go to www.GodistheIssue.com and download the small group Bible study based on this book. I have heard many people say after reading this book, "We need to do that." However, in our initial tests after people completed the eight-week small group Bible study, what I have often heard is, "I think differently now." *Thinking differently is the key.* Any time you are dealing with a new paradigm, it usually takes some time to really let it sink in and penetrate your thinking. You have to kick it around a bit. And it is helpful to see how Jesus, Paul, Peter and others used this paradigm to advance the gospel. The key to change is learning to think differently.

Those are the four basic areas each of us must master if we are to be conduits of real change for the culture around us. However, changing our own thinking is only the first (albeit, critical) step. The second step is helping others to change. Therefore, after you complete each step (whatever order you chose) with your cell group, encourage each member of the group to go out and replicate that step of the process with other friends. There is no need to wait until the end of the process. Maybe two can start a new group together. It is generally helpful to have a friend with you when you are doing something for the first time. And once you have gone through the entire process with this cell group start another cell group.

Keep this up and after a few years the exponential effect will begin to kick in. Let me explain briefly. If this year you coach four people, then by the end of the year you will have multiplied yourself four times over. But then the second year have each of those four start their own cell groups as well (each with four people). By the end of that second year you will have trained 16 people. Follow this process the third year and you will have trained 64 people. The fourth year you will have replicated yourself 256 times just through the first group alone. After five years it will be over 1,000. Keep this process up for fifty years and… Well, I think you get the idea.

I grew up around Campus Crusade for Christ. We always called the above scenario the "multiplication" process summed up by the words, *"Win, Build, Send."* Empowered by the Spirit of God, we would *Win* a person to Jesus Christ, *Build* them in their faith, then *Send* them out to repeat the same process with someone else. It is a very simple but highly effective strategy.

The ripple effect of your efforts is what will change America.

For instance, we began working in South Korea in 1958 (fifty years ago). At the time the Christian population was very small. Today, over half of the people in South Korea claim to be Christian, and now, they are sending people throughout the globe as missionaries—especially to countries very difficult for people from the West to penetrate. Did Campus Crusade for Christ do all this? No. We helped get the ball rolling, but the multiplication process did the rest. I could give you many other examples. The process works in real life. And, of course, it was the primary means of building the first century Church.

The ripple effect of your efforts is what will change America (and ultimately, the world). And the great thing is you do not need Hollywood, Wall Street or Washington, D.C in order to succeed. All you need is to find a few like-minded or at least open-minded friends and get started.

Just an encouraging reminder—again: you cannot eat the entire elephant today. You will not move Mt. Everest in a week. You will not build the Great Wall of China in a month. But in a lifetime—you can go a long way if you go together with others. Keep on taking baby steps each day—but *always* with the final goal in mind. That is the path to victory. That is what births dramatic change. History may not remember you, but have no doubt, history itself will be changed as a result.

Keep on taking baby steps each day—but always with the final goal in mind. That is the path to victory.

I cannot promise you that we will turn American culture around. Only God knows the future. I cannot even promise that we will make God the central issue in American society. But I can promise you that if we do not try we will not succeed. I can promise you, *if we fail to make God the issue, we shall most certainly and inevitably fail at all other related tasks.* And I can promise that as you pursue knowing Him and making Him the issue your life will never be the same.

In the end, there are really only two choices. As I said in Chapter 1, we can "cry at the grave of God"[69] with Friedrich Nietzsche, or we can worship at the manger with the wise men and the shepherds. The tide is flowing against us. May God grant us wisdom, courage, and strength for the journey ahead. May He grant us the privilege of helping our fellow Americans once again rediscover the God of the Bible. May He grant that America once again be transformed into a shining light on a hill. And may God Bless America once again.

END NOTES

Chapter 1

1. George Washington, from his Farewell Address, September 19, 1796. Quoted in James D. Richardson, *A Compilation of the Messages and Papers of the Presidents, 1789–1897* (Published by Authority of Congress, 1899), Vol. I, p. 220.

2. Quoted in *America's God and Country Encyclopedia of Quotations*, compiled by William J. Federer (St. Louis, MO: FAME Publishing, 1999), p. 660.

3. John Adams in his address to the military, October 11, 1798. Quoted in Charles Francis Adams, ed., *The Works of John Adams—Second President of the United States* (Boston: Little, Brown, & Co., 1854), Vol. IX, p. 229.

4. Jane Clayson interview with Anne Graham Lotz, "The Early Show," September 13, 2001 (www.cbsnews.com/earlyshow/healthwatch/healthnews/20010913terror_spiritual.shtml).

5. Margaret Sanger from her personal writings. Quoted in Bill Bright, *Red Sky in the Morning* (New Life Resources), p. 94.

6. Aldous Huxley, *Ends and Means* (Harper & Brothers, 1927), p. 315. Quoted by Os Guinness in *Time for Truth* (Grand Rapids, MI: Baker Books, 2002), p. 113.

7. Aleksandr Solzhenitsyn, "Warning to the West," delivered over the BBC radio network, March 24, 1976.

8. The illustration of patching the walls of the house was from a talk by Rev. Tony Evans at Campus Crusade for Christ's 1992 U.S. Staff Training conference.

9. Lest my words be misconstrued, I am not espousing a theocracy in any way, shape, or form. "Christianity" imposed by fiat, rather than freely embraced, is not Christianity at all. It would in fact be no better than the militant Islamic theocracies that enforce and advance outward adherence to Islam by the ruthless wielding of the sword.

10. Using a process called "linkage" (which I discuss in Chapter 3), the press has effectively linked the concept of stem-cell research with the use of embryos to find cures for various diseases. In reality, no such cures have come from the use of embryonic stem cells; on the contrary, all successes to date have been through the use of stem cells from adults or other nondestructive sources.

11. Steven Butts, "Pornography: A Serious Cultural Disorder That is Accelerating," *Lancaster Sunday News*, March 9, 1997. Quoted by James Dobson in *Bringing Up Boys* (Wheaton, IL: Tyndale House Publishers, 2001), p. 210.

12. George Barna, "Americans Are Most Likely to Base Truth on Feelings," *Barna Update*, Feb. 12, 2002.

13. George Barna, *Real Teens* (Ventura, CA: Regal Books, 2001), p. 131.

14. Ibid., p. 124.

15. Ibid., p. 132.

16. "2002 Report Card: The Ethics of American Youth," Josephson Institute of Ethics, October 20–26, 2002.

17. Ibid.

18. Oswald Chambers, *My Utmost for His Highest* (Westwood, NJ: Barbour & Company, Inc., 1935), p. 96.

19. Friedrich Nietzsche, *The Gay Science* (1882, 1887) para. 124; Walter Kaufmann ed. (New York: Vintage, 1974), pp. 181-82.

20. Ibid

21. Tammy Bruce, *The Death of Right and Wrong* (Roseville, CA: Prima Publishing, 2003) p.11

22. Gary Wolf, "The Church of the Non-Believers," <u>Wired</u>, Issue 14.11, November 2006.

23. Cathy Lynn Grossman, "View of God can reveal your values and politics", <u>USA TODAY</u>, September 12, 2006, sec 1A, p. 1.

24. This quote is commonly attributed to Nietzsche which is why I have used it, but so far I have been unable to confirm or refute the veracity of such attribution

Chapter 3

25. Denise Keirnan, "Christian group won't allow gay student to be leaders," *The Daily of the University of Washington*, October 13, 1994, p. 1.

26. Jim Brünner, "Why is CCC's discrimination condoned by UW?" *The Daily of the University of Washington*, October 14, 1994, p. 4.

27. Martin Luther King, Jr., *Strength to Love* (Fortress, NY: Fortress Press, 1963).

28. Joseph Lieberman, from his address at Notre Dame University, October 24, 2000. Aired on *The News Hour with Jim Lehrer* on PBS on October 26, 2000.

29. "American Faith is Diverse, As Shown Among Five Faith-Based Segments," *The Barna Report*, January 29, 2002 (www.barna.org).

Chapter 4

30. Speech at the *Harrow School*, October 29, 1941.
31. Bill Bright and Ron Jenson, *Kingdoms at War* (San Bernardino, CA: Here's Life Publishers, 1986), pp. 28–29.
32. Philippians 1:21 (NIV)
33. Technically, they are "Positive Law" jurists who by definition believe that law is based solely upon prior law (case law) rather than on right and wrong. Therefore, in order to change law all they need do is find an obscure law or court decision that can be interpreted to show precedent for their view. Right and wrong, and by implication justice, have nothing to do with it.
34. Acts 17:23 (NIV)
35. Acts 4:19
36. The only exception to this rule I can think of is in Acts 24:24-25, when Paul was testifying before the Roman ruler Festus (whose wife was Jewish) talking about "faith in Jesus, righteousness and self-control" - the latter term clearly implying behavior.
37. Saul D. Alinsky, *Rules for Radicals: A Pragmatic Primer for Realistic Radicals* (Vintage Books, 1989), p.136.
38. "One bite at a time."
39. One step at a time.
40. The U.S. economy went from a stall into overdrive. The Soviet empire collapsed due to its inability to compete economically.
41. Luke 22:44
42. Acts 5:40-41
43. Acts 11:23-27
44. See Acts 4:16-21; Acts 5:28-41; Acts 12:1-5; Church tradition says he was crucified upside down.
45. Romans 9:1-3
46. Winston Churchill is widely regarded as having made this statement. However, I have been unable to find the source document.
47. In the Continental Congress just before signing the Declaration of Independence, 1776
48. See Matthew 21:1-3; Mark 6:7; Mark 14:13; Luke 10:1; Matthew 18:19.
49. John 13:27
50. NLT

Chapter 5

51. John 13:34 (NLT)
52. New Living Translation
53. Quoted in *America's God and Country Encyclopedia of Quotations*, compiled by William J. Federer (St. Louis, MO: FAME Publishing, 1996), p. 676.
54. BBC News, "Erfurt massacre planned for months," April 30, 2002.
55. BBC News, "History of School Shootings," April 26, 2002.
56. According to abcNEWS.com, September 25, 2001, Cassie Bernall's friend, Michelle Fox, said, "Cassie was in the library studying the Bible, as she did every day at lunch, when the shooting began. She knelt and prayed, which angered one of the shooters. But she continued to pray, so he shot her. 'I know she died because of her faith in God.'"
57. Luke 6:27
58. Quoted in *America's God and Country Encyclopedia of Quotations*, p. 540.
59. Mr. Blair was finally forced to resign May 1, 2003, only after the evidence was becoming too public to suppress any longer. This, of course, raises the question of how many other reporters working for the *Times* engage in similar behavior since the *Times* seems to ave a rather indulgent lack of enforcement of their own purported standards. It is one thing to work with a reporter who makes an "honest mistake." But continuing to trust a known liar to report the truth makes no sense.
60. This argument also applies directly to the euthanasia (death with dignity/mercy killing) debate.
61. In most cases I would recommend bringing in someone from the outside to debate, since this is not a subject that most high school students are well equipped to handle.
62. Mein Kampf.
63. Thomas Jefferson, November 16, 1798, in the Kentucky Resolutions of 1798, Article III. Quoted in America's God and Country Encyclopedia of Quotations, p. 323.
64. For more quotes by Thomas Jefferson regarding Church and State issues, see *America's God and Country Encyclopedia of Quotations*.
65. Joseph Lieberman, address at Notre Dame University, October 24, 2000. Aired on *The News Hour with Jim Lehrer* on PBS on October 26, 2000.
66. This quote is widely attributed to Benjamin Franklin, but I have so far been unable to confirm it..

Chapter 6

67. This exchange is not literally verbatim word for word, but it is pretty close. It faithfully represents the essence of the conversation.

68. Tom Carter, comp., 2200 Quotations from the writings of Charles H. Spurgeon. (Grand Rapids, MI: Baker Books, 1988), pp. 101-2.

69. This quote is commonly attributed to Nietzsche which is why I have used it, but so far I have been unable to confirm or refute the veracity of such attribution.

About the Author

BRAD BRIGHT is the youngest son of Bill and Vonette Bright, founders of Campus Crusade for Christ. Shortly after graduating from Wheaton College, Brad entered national politics as a result of both Watergate and studying the life of William Wilberforce. He worked as an aide to U.S. Senator William Armstrong of Colorado, as a deputy director of the National Republican Congressional Committee, and as director of a foundation to promote volunteerism as an alternative to federal government programs. In 1989 he joined the staff of Campus Crusade for Christ, where he has worked with both college students and national leaders. He is President and CEO of Bright Media Foundation, and serves as the director of a strategy called "Discover God" which seeks to reframe the God-concept of both Christians and non-Christians in America today. He resides in Orlando, Florida, with his wife, Kathy, and their two children.

"Brad Bright understands that we need to think strategically in the culture war. How we communicate is just as important as what we believe. Brad captures this in his book."

J.C. Watts, Jr.
Former Congressman

"Brad Bright has written a book for those who want to bring positive change to American culture. He peels away the superficial layers that encase the core issue of our times and reveals that the most important issue is God Himself. A highly committed group of individuals can do much to bring God back to the fore of culture discussion, and reading this book might just motivate you to become one of those individuals. In this book, it's back to the basic idea that God is the issue, to which we can all shout a hearty 'Amen!'"

Alan Sears
CCEO and General Counsel, Alliance Defense Fund

"*God is the Issue* is a must-read for Christians who are serious about making a difference in their world and impacting their culture. Brad clearly grasps the reality that God—not simply the Church—is at the heart of the Christian worldview! The principles found here give practical handles for how to biblically stand and be counted in the midst of a confused and conflicted culture."

Dr. Robert E. Reccord
President, North American Mission Board, Southern Baptist Convention

---

"Is it time for a paradigm shift on the part of the people of God? Brad Bright thinks so and makes a compelling case for it in his new book, God is the Issue. To reach the lost and to redeem the culture more effectively will take a renewed effort and a renewed mind. This intriguing book shows the way."

Dr. D. James Kennedy
Sr. Pastor, Coral Ridge Presbyterian Church, Ft. Lauderdale, Florida

---

"Anyone who believes they can restore 'traditional values' in America without first restoring the foundation of those values, God Himself, needs to read this book before they proceed any further. Brad Bright makes a compelling case for a new kind of activism in America."

Dr. Pat Robertson
Chairman & CEO, The Christian Broadcasting Network, Inc.